The Easy Guide to Accounting and Bookkeeping Terms for Small Business

Karen Matthews

First published by Easy Accounts Pty Ltd 2020
Copyright © 2020 Karen Matthews

ISBN 978-0-646-81259-5

Karen Matthews has asserted her right under the Copyright, Designs and Patents Act 1988 to be identified as author of this work. The information in this book is based on the author's experiences and opinions. The publisher specifically disclaims responsibility for any adverse consequences, which may result from use of the information contained herein. Permission to use information has been sought by the author. Any breaches will be rectified in further editions of the book.

This publication is designed to provide an easy guide to common accounting and bookkeeping terms for small business. It is sold on the understanding that neither the author or the publisher is engaged in rendering, accounting, legal, or other professional advice. If accounting or other expert assistance is required for your specific situation, the services of a relevant professional person should be sought.

All rights reserved. No part of this publication may be reproduced in any form whatsoever without the prior written permission of the author. Any enquires should be made through the publisher.

Easy Accounts Pty Ltd
P O Box 3242
Robina Queensland
Australia 4226

Testimonials

"I needed to gain an understanding of accounting and bookkeeping terms and this book is perfect. I enjoy having it near-by, to make sure I gain an understanding of what various terms mean. I highly recommend it to all small business owners and others."

Helen Cooper, Next Gen

"A must have book for an easy guide to commonly encountered accounting and bookkeeping terms. I keep this in my office and refer to it often. It has helped me to gain a better understanding of many terms used in business."

James Perkins, Investor

"This book is concise and user friendly. I learnt the real meaning of many accounting terms I had heard before and that there are sometimes different terms used that mean the same. The book is relevant and a definite go to in my business. I highly recommend it."

Brett Robertson

Dedication

Thank you to my family, friends and mentors. I am forever grateful for your support and encouragement to write and share this book.

Contents

Welcome! ix

Chapter 1: A Terms 1

Chapter 2: B Terms 11

Chapter 3: C Terms 17

Chapter 4: D Terms 29

Chapter 5: E Terms 37

Chapter 6: F Terms 43

Chapter 7: G Terms 47

Chapter 8: H Terms 51

Chapter 9: I Terms 53

Chapter 10: J Terms 59

Chapter 11: K Terms 61

Chapter 12: L Terms 63

Chapter 13: M Terms 67

Chapter 14: N Terms 71

Chapter 15: O Terms 75

Chapter 16: P Terms 79

Chapter 17: Q Terms 87

Chapter 18: R Terms 89

Chapter 19: S Terms 95

Chapter 20: T Terms 105

Chapter 21: U Terms 111

Chapter 22: V Terms 115

Chapter 23: W Terms 117

Chapter 24: X Terms 121

Chapter 25: Y Terms 123

Chapter 26: Z Terms 125

About The Author 129

Let's Get Social 130

Bibliography 131

Free Cash Flow Forecast Spreadsheet!! 135

Online Bookkeeping Course 137

WELCOME!

Welcome!

Congratulations on choosing this book and taking another step towards understanding accounting and bookkeeping terms commonly encountered in small business.

During my years of accounting I've often heard statements such as "I need to understand your world better.", "I get confused between what is a debtor and a creditor." or "I have no idea what those 'things' are or mean on my financial statements." As a teenager, I too remember thinking similar when looking at the financial statements of my parents small business. What did all those numbers mean?

In business, it is important to know and understand your numbers. This enables you to see where the business has been, where it is at and where the business is heading.

The rapid advances in technology have provided the tools to make this easier, more efficient, timely and more user friendly than ever before.

Gaining knowledge of common accounting and bookkeeping terms is a first step towards understanding your numbers. With chapters from A-Z this book provides an easy guide to help you demystify and learn the jargon of the accounting and bookkeeping world.

Let's begin.

CHAPTER 1

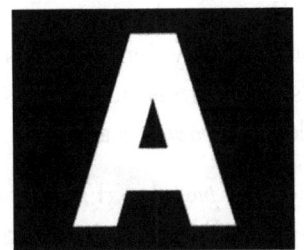

TERMS

aba file: Australian Banking Association (aba) file is a standard file used by Australian banks to specify payments to be made from one bank account to one or more bank accounts. For example, it is used for uploading multiple bills for payment or employers to pay employees via an *aba file* which can be generated by their payroll software. See **batch payments processing.**

abnormal expenses: are expenses that are unusual or irregular and aren't part of your everyday business, such as lawsuit. See **extraordinary item.**

account: in accounting refers to either:

i) the place in the *general ledger* where business transactions of a similar nature are recorded. For example, the 'stationery account' is where all similar payments for stationery items such as paper, pens, paper clips are recorded, the 'subscriptions account' is where all subscription payments are recorded. An *account* is also called a **ledger account.**

It lists all the transactions *posted* to that account either as a *debit* or a *credit,* the date, transaction details and amount. A running total of the account balance is automatically shown when using accounting software.

A list of all the account names is called the chart of accounts. See **general ledger, chart of accounts.**

ii) the individual accounts the business has for accounts payable (creditors) and accounts receivable (debtors), or bank, credit cards or other financial accounts.

account balance: is the current total of an account. For example:

i) **general ledger accounts** – the account balance of an account is the sum of the opening balance and all the debits and credits posted to that account.

ii) **bank account** - in banking, an account balance is the current cash balance in a cheque, savings, credit card or other financial account.

account classification: there are five main account classifications: Assets, Liabilities, Equity, Revenue (Income) and Expenses. All ledger accounts are listed under one of these. For example: a stationery account is an expense account.

account code: or general ledger code, is a number used to record business transactions to an account in the general ledger.

accounts: financial statements can be referred to as the accounts or annual accounts. See *financial statements.*

accounting: focuses on the review, interpreting, classifying, analysing, reporting and summarising of the financial data of the business. Accounting typically consists of preparation of financial statements and reports, budgets, tax returns, analysing business performance, business advisory services. Some accountants also provide bookkeeping services. See *bookkeeping.*

accounting cycle: is all the accounting procedures from processing transactions that occur in a business to providing the business results in the form of financial statements or other reports to management and other related parties.

accounting entity: the business for which accounting records are maintained and for which financial statements are prepared. The *separate entity concept* regards the business as a separate entity from its owner. The business financial transactions are recorded separately from those of the owner.

accounting equation: the double entry method of accounting is based on the accounting equation which is:

Assets = Liabilities + Equity *or the extended version:*

Assets + Expenses = Liabilities + Equity + Revenue

Assets, Liabilities and Equity represent Balance Sheet accounts.

Revenue and Expenses are Income Statement accounts. See *double entry accounting.*

accounting period: See *reporting period.*

accounting records: manual or computerised records of assets and liabilities, various journals, ledgers, monetary transactions (including payroll records) and all supporting *source documents* which a business is required to keep for certain number of years. The business's accounting records are also referred to as the ***books.***

accounts list: see *chart of accounts.*

accounts payable: money that you owe to suppliers. Unpaid supplier invoices/bills (money owed by the business to other businesses) are grouped under the accounts payable control account.

See ***creditor, trade creditors, payables.***

accounts payable control account: is an account in the general ledger used to *record summary transactions* relating to *accounts payable*. The balance on the accounts payable control account reflects the amount of bills outstanding that the business *owes* its suppliers for *credit sales*.

The accounts payable control account is also referred to as ***creditors control account*** or simply *creditors* or *accounts payable* or *trade payables control account* or *payables control account,* depending on the setup of your accounting system. See ***accounts payable ledger.***

accounts payable ledger: is a subsidiary ledger that lists all the suppliers and their account balances that a business owes money to. Common abbreviation: *A/P ledger.* The accounts payable ledger is also referred to as the ***creditors ledger*** or ***payables ledger.*** See ***subsidiary ledger.***

accounts receivable: the money which is *owed to you* by your *customers*. Unpaid sales invoices (money owed to the business by customers) are grouped under accounts receivable control account. See ***debtor, trade debtors, receivables.***

accounts receivable control account: is an *account* in the general ledger used to *record summary transactions* relating to *accounts receivable*. The balance on the accounts receivable control account reflects the amount outstanding of invoices *owed* to the business by its customers for *credit sales*.

The accounts receivable control account is also referred to as **debtors control account** or simply *debtors* or *accounts receivable* depending on the setup of your accounting system. See **accounts receivable ledger.**

accounts receivable ledger: is a subsidiary ledger that lists all the customers and their account balances that is <u>owed to</u> the business. Common Abbrev: *A/R ledger.* The accounts receivable ledger is also called the **debtors ledger.** See **subsidiary ledger.**

accounts receivable turnover ratio: measures how many times a business can collect its average accounts receivable during the year. A high receivables turnover ratio can indicate that a company's collection of accounts receivable is efficient. The accounts receivable turnover is calculated by dividing net credit sales by average accounts receivable.:

$$\text{Accounts Receivable Turnover} = \frac{\text{Net Credit Sales}}{\text{Average Accounts Receivable}}$$

accrual accounting: an accounting method where *revenues* and *expenses* are *recorded as they are incurred*, no matter when cash is received.

Revenue is recorded in the financial statements at the time the sale occurs, regardless of when you receive cash from a customer, and you record expenses at the time you receive a bill from a supplier, regardless of when you pay this bill.

For example: The business buys supplies in April, receives the invoice and only pays the invoice in May. The purchase is recorded and shown on the Profit and Loss Statement in April, at the date of the invoice, not in May when it was paid. Accrual accounting is also referred to as **accrual-basis accounting.** See **matching principle, cash accounting.**

accrued expenses: the expenses a business has incurred but not yet paid for at the time the business closes its accounting books for the period to prepare its financial statements. For example: accrual for advertising, electricity, legal fees, wages earned by employees but not paid at year-end.

accumulated amortisation: the amount of amortisation that has been accumulated on an intangible asset since it was purchased.

accumulated depreciation: the amount of depreciation that has been accumulated on a fixed asset since it was purchased.

acid test ratio: See *current ratio.*

add, edit or remove an account: functions in your accounting software to customise the accounts in the chart of accounts, as required, to suit your business needs. See *account.*

add-ons: in accounting are additional apps a business can choose to install to add additional features, to your online accounting software. See *app.*

adjusting journal entries: used to adjust records directly without changing individual transactions. Common adjustments include depreciation, amortisation, accrued expense liabilities.

adjustment note: See *credit note.*

administration: is when a company becomes insolvent and is put under the management of an administrator, who must be a registered liquidator. Either directors or creditors can appoint administrators through a court process in order to protect the company and their position as much as possible. See *voluntary administration, involuntary administration.*

aged payables report: a report that lists how much money *you owe to suppliers,* grouped according to how *old the bills* are.

aged receivables report: a report that lists how much each *customer owes you,* grouped according to how *old the debts* are.

allocate: to apportion or assign a debit or credit to appropriate accounts. An allocation can be between accounts or between periods of time.

amortise: to reduce the value of an *intangible asset* by a certain percentage each year to show that it's being used up.

annual report: a document prepared each year by a public company, to inform shareholders and other potential investors, about its activities and financial performance. The report includes audited financial statements. See ***financial statements.***

antivirus software: programs designed to prevent, detect and remove viruses from your computing devices.

app: is a software application most often used in reference to a mobile app (for mobile devices - smartphone, tablets) or a small piece of software that runs on a website. In accounting some apps are referred to as *add-ons* as they can also be synced to your online accounting software to further increase efficiencies in a various areas of the business. There are currently over 700 apps offered for various functions including document management, crm, inventory, payments, payroll, time tracking etc.

Sometimes apps are referred to as horizontal or vertical. A horizontal app works across all types of businesses. A vertical app is specific to a particular industry or business type.

app stack: is the various software and tools used in your business. Typical app stacks include closely related apps that aid in the completion of a certain tasks. An app stack is also referred to as ***application stack, technology stack, tech stack.*** See ***add on.***

archive: saving data and other records for safekeeping because it is important information that is likely to be used again in the future.

arm's length transaction: a transaction that involves a buyer and a seller who can act independently of each other and have no financial relationship with each other.

asset retirement: is when an asset is permanently removed from use in the business. Asset retirement can occur in processes such as a sale to another party or disposal due to obsolescence.

assets: items of value owned by a business. Assets are reported on the balance sheet and include current assets like cash, money in bank accounts, cash in petty cash box, accounts receivable and non-current assets like equipment, land and buildings, motor vehicles, patents. See *current assets, non-current assets, intangible assets.*

assets useful life: See **effective life of an asset.**

audit: is an independent examination and verification of the assets, liabilities, financial transactions and controls of a company, to determine the reliability of its accounting records. This enables the auditor to form an independent opinion about the accuracy of the company's financial statements.

audit proofing: a business will need to provide proof of financial transactions and other records as requested by the ATO or other related parties. The essentials to audit proofing a business is to ensure your record keeping is outstanding. This usually *includes* the use of online accounting software, copies of all source documents for income and expenses, a motor vehicle log book (as required), maintaining home office records (as required), detailed records of business travel, seeking help of a qualified accountant, tax advisor or bookkeeper. See *source documents.*

audit report: a letter from the auditors stating their opinion on the financial information provided and whether the financial statements have been completed in accordance with generally accepted accounting principles.

audit trail: the records and source documents that enables accounting entries to be tracked back to their source. See *transaction trail.*

Australian Accounting Standards (AASs): are technical financial standards that set out the required accounting measurements and disclosures for particular types of material transactions and events. See *Australian Accounting Standards Board (AASB).*

Australian Accounting Standards Board (AASB): is an Australian government agency that develops and maintains financial reporting standards applicable to entities in the private and public sectors of the Australian economy.

Australian Bureau of Statistics (ABS): the Australian governments statistical agency, proving official statistics on a wide range of economic, social, population and environmental matters of importance to Australia.

Australian Business Number (ABN): is a unique eleven-digit number issued by the Australian Tax Office (ATO), that identifies your business to the government and community. An ABN doesn't replace your tax file number, but is used for various tax and other business purposes. See *Tax File Number (TFN)*.

Australian Company Number (CAN): is a unique nine-digit number issued by the Australian Securities and Investment Commission (ASIC) to every company when registered as an identifier.

Australian Competition and Consumer Commission (ACCC): is an independent Commonwealth statutory authority whose role is to enforce the *Competition and Consumer Act 2010* and a range of additional legislation, promoting competition, fair trading and regulating national infrastructure for the benefit of all Australians.

Australian Securities and Investment Commission (ASIC): is an independent Australian government body that acts as Australia's corporate regulator. The Australian Securities and Investments Commission's role is to enforce and regulate company and financial services laws to protect Australian consumers, investors and creditors.

Australian Taxation Office (ATO): is the principal revenue collection agency of the Australian Government. The ATO has responsibility for administering the Australian federal taxation system, superannuation legislation, and other associated matters.

authenticator app: provides a one-time, time based, numeric *passcode* that's used as an extra security step during the login process. It means if someone guesses or knows your password, it's not enough to access your account. Search for "authenticator" in your app store. See *two-step authentication (2SA)*.

authorised signatory: on a cheque, is a person or persons whom the bank has on record as being authorised by an entity to sign their cheques. Sometimes cheques need to be jointly signed by two of the authorised signatories.

auto-fetch: a function in a document management software that can be enabled to allow the software to automatically receive documents such as invoices or statements from the banks and online suppliers. See *document management software, paperless office.*

automation: is the technology by which a process or procedure is performed with minimal human assistance.

awards: modern awards are legal documents that outline the minimum pay rates and conditions of employment. There are more than 100 industry or occupation awards that cover most people who work in Australia. See *the fair work commission (FWC), the fair work ombudsman (FWO).*

CHAPTER 2

TERMS

backlog: an amount of work that has built up and needs to be completed. For example, it can refer to sales orders still waiting to be filled or the business paperwork that needs to be processed. See ***back order.***

back order: is an order for a good or service that cannot be filled at the current time due to a lack of available supply. See ***backlog.***

backup: an extra electronic copy of computer data that is stored elsewhere. This could be to a password protected portable storage drive or online storage such as dropbox or goggle drive. Backups are vital to preventing loss of data if the computer crashes, is stolen or becomes infected with ransomware. See ***cyberattack.***

bad debts: an *amount owing* from a *customer* that you know isn't going to be paid. The sales invoices have been written off because the payments are *significantly overdue and never likely to be paid*. Sales invoices are only written off after some effort to retrieve the funds including going through debt collection agencies.

balance sheet: the financial statement that provides a snapshot, as at a *fixed date* in time, of the value of *assets* the business owns, what the business owes in *liabilities* and how much *equity* is in the business. The balance sheet is also referred to as the ***statement of financial position.***

bank: the secure financial institution where businesses deposit their earnings and from which they pay their bills.

bank feeds: the process whereby your accounting software can be linked to your bank to automatically download a list of the transactions from your nominated bank account into your online accounting software. This enables matching of a transaction in the bank feed with a sales invoice awaiting collection, a bill awaiting payment or other expenses paid, ready for you to review.

bank reconciliation: a report showing the reconciled difference between the bank account balance in the general ledger, with the bank's information on the bank statement. See ***reconciliation.***

bank rules: rules that you configure in your online accounting software to recognise certain kinds of transactions and allocate these transactions correctly.

bankruptcy: is the legal procedure for liquidating a business (or property owned by an individual) who is unable to pay their creditors. Bankruptcies can be categorised into two types: (1) *voluntary bankruptcy* where the insolvent business initiates it themselves, or (2) *involuntary bankruptcy* where it can be forced on court orders issued on a creditors petition, with the aim to seek payment through an equitable distribution of the business's assets. See *insolvent, liquidation.*

bank statement: a periodic statement, usually monthly, produced by the bank which lists the opening balance then in date order, all the money received and all the money paid out of the bank account, ending with the closing balance of cash in the account.

bas: See *business activity statement (BAS).*

bas agent: an individual or an entity licensed by the Tax Practitioners Board to provide bas services. (Australia Only) See *bas services.*

bas services: any bookkeeping activity related to GST or PAYG, including configuring tax codes in accounting software, coding tax invoices, preparing business activity statements. (Australia only)

batch payments processing: used to bundle multiple bills that you need to pay into one payment transaction, by creating a payment file and using internet banking to upload the file to your bank account for payment. See *aba file.*

bills: a digital, printed or written document of the money owed to a supplier for goods or services. See *invoice.*

billing: invoicing customers for goods or services they have purchased from the business. Billing is also referred to as *invoicing.*

bitcoin: is a digital and global money system currency. It allows people to exchange money across the internet without being linked to a real identity. See *cryptocurrency.*

black economy: refers to a commercial activity that operates outside the tax and other regulatory systems such as welfare and migration. Black economy behaviours include: demanding or paying for work cash in hand to avoid obligations, not reporting or under-reporting income, visa fraud, identity fraud, sham contracting, money laundering. The black economy is also referred to as *the shadow economy, the underground economy, or the informal economy.*

board meeting: a formal, usually monthly, meeting of a company's directors (board members) to discuss business performance and future direction of the company. See *boardroom, director.*

boardroom: a room reserved for regular meetings of company directors.

bookkeeping: focuses on recording and organising financial data. Bookkeeping typically consists of day-to-day roles for payroll, invoicing, receipts and bills, filing, recording business transactions. See *accounting.*

books: a term to mean the business's accounting records.

book value: or carrying value is the net worth of an asset that is recorded on the balance sheet. It is calculated by subtracting any accumulated depreciation form an asset's purchase price. Book value can also be thought of as the net asset value of a company calculated as total assets minus intangible assets (patents, goodwill) and liabilities. See *written-down value.*

boom: is the period that follows the recovery phase in a standard economic cycle. It is characterised by an economy working at full capacity, strong consumer demand, low rate of unemployment and a rising stock market, usually accompanied by rapidly increasing consumer prices. See *economic cycle.*

bottom line: is the final result. The term comes from the layout of the profit and loss statement, in which the bottom line shows the extent of the profit or loss after all income and expenses have been taken into account. See *profit.*

bounce: of a cheque, means to be dishonoured. A bank declines to pay the amount on the cheque, usually because the drawer's account has insufficient funds. The cheque is returned to the person who presented it, endorsed 'refer to drawer'. See *cheque.*

break-even point: the point at which total revenues equals total expenses.

budget: a financial plan which estimates revenues and expenditure for a future period of time (eg for the year ahead). The actual figures are then regularly monitored against this plan.

business: is the activity of making one's living or making money by producing or buying and selling products such as goods and services.

business activity statement (BAS): is a form submitted to the Australian Taxation Office (ATO) by businesses that are registered for GST to report their tax obligations, including GST, pay as you go withholding, pay as you go instalments, fringe benefits tax, wine equalisation tax an luxury car tax. See *instalment activity statement (IAS).*

business cycle: See *economic cycle.*

business plan: is a written document that sets out a plan from a marketing, financial and operational viewpoint of how the business is going to achieve its goals within a set time frame.

CHAPTER 3

TERMS

calendar year: is always 1 January to 31 December. A *fiscal year*, by contrast, can start and end at any point during the year, as long as it comprises a full twelve months. A company that starts its fiscal year on 1 January and ends it on 31 December operates on a calendar year basis. See ***fiscal year.***

capital: the financial assets such as funds held in deposit accounts or funds obtained from debt or equity financing so that the business can operate and grow. Capital can also refer to the capital assets of company. See ***working capital, equity capital, debt.***

capital asset: is a tangible asset with a useful life longer than a year that is not intended for sale in the regular course of the business's operation.

capital expenditure: outlay of money to buy or improve capital assets, such as equipment, buildings and factories.

capital gain: the profits a company makes when it sells a capital asset for more than it originally paid for that asset.

capital improvement: expenditure that increases the asset value. This cost is added to the asset value and depreciated.

capital introduced: the personal funds or assets a business owner introduces to the business so it can operate.

capital loss: a capital loss occurs when you dispose of a capital asset for less than its tax value.

cash accounting: an accounting method where revenues and expenses are only recorded when cash changes hands.

Revenue is recorded in the financial statements when you receive cash from a customer, and you only record expenses when you pay cash to a supplier.

For example: the business buys supplies in April, receives the invoice dated April and pays the invoice in May. The purchase is recorded and show on the Income Statement in May, the date the invoice was paid. Cash accounting is also referred to as ***cash-basis accounting.*** See ***accrual accounting.***

cash book: a book used in a *manual accounting system*, where all funds moving in (cash receipts) and out (cash payments) of the business through the bank account are recorded in chronological order. The cash book columns should contain the following transaction detail: date, reference, transaction description, total amount, GST (if applicable), columns to record the net amount for income and expense items with room at the top and bottom of each page to show the beginning and ending balances for the month.

cash book balance: the bank statement balance adjusted for any uncleared deposits or withdrawals.

cash flow: the amount of money that moves into and out of a business. See *statement of cash flows.*

cash flow forecast: an accounting report showing *estimations* of the income and expenses for the year ahead. This helps a business plan the projected cash requirements needed, month by month, for the year ahead.

cash flow from operations: cash a company receives from the day-to-day operations of the business, usually from sales of products or services.

cash payments journal: a *special journal* used to record all cash payments such as cash purchases and cash paid to creditors. Cash payments could be made via cheques, credit card, EFTPOS or cash. See *cash transaction, special journals.*

cash receipts journal: a *special journal* used to record all cash receipts such as payments received from cash sales, funds received from debtors. Cash receipts could be made via cheques, credit card, EFTPOS or cash. See *cash transaction special journals.*

cash transaction: transactions where you get paid, or make a payment, at the time of the transaction are referred to as cash transactions. This is not limited to transactions where actual dollars and cents change hands, but also transactions involving payments by credit card, EFTPOS or cheque. See *credit transaction.*

chart of accounts: the list of accounts set up in an accounting system into which you allocate financial transactions. The list of accounts is typically shown in the order the accounts appear in its financial statements. Traditionally the balance sheet accounts (assets, liabilities, equity) appear first followed by the income statement accounts (revenue (income) and expenses).

chattel mortgage: a form of finance where ownership transfers to the purchaser right from the start.

checklist: is a list of items required, things to be done, or points to be considered. It helps to ensure consistency and completeness in carrying out a task.

cheque: is a special pre-printed slip of paper produced by the bank, containing the business name, bank account details and a unique cheque number. They are usually provided in a cheque book and used by a business to make payments instead of using cash or online banking.

A cheque is completed by entering the date, the name of the person/business being paid and the amount to be paid in both word and numeric value. The cheque requires the signature of the person/s who are an authorised signatory of the bank account from which the cheque is issued. With the increased use of online banking, cheques are becoming less common. See *cheque book.*

cheque book: is a book of cheques produced by the bank and used by a business to make payments. Each cheque has a corresponding cheque butt.

cheque butt: is the left side of a cheque book that is left behind once a cheque has been filled out and removed from the cheque book. It is used to record all the details of the cheque – the date of payment, the name of the person being paid, description of item being paid and the amount. The cheque butt has the same cheque number printed on it as the cheque.

cleared funds: the proceeds of cheques and other types of payment that have become available for withdrawal after a specified waiting period. The length of the waiting period is determined by the beneficiary's bank and can also depend on the type of payment involved. For example: the proceeds of electronic transfers become cleared funds more quickly than cheques. See *uncleared funds.*

clearing account: is an account, in the general ledger, containing costs or amounts that are to be transferred to another account. For example, an 'undeposited funds' account is used as a clearing account for payments/money that has been received but not yet deposited into the business bank account. See *undeposited funds.*

closing month of accounting year: is the last month of your accounting year or tax year. An accounting or tax year is usually twelve consecutive months, based on either a calendar year or a fiscal year. See *fiscal year.*

cloud: is the online space where you can access your data. A network of servers find what data you need and deliver it. See *cloud accounting, servers.*

cloud accounting: is using cloud (online) accounting software to store and work on your accounts in the cloud (online) rather than storing your data on a desktop computer or server in your office. See *cloud accounting software.*

cloud accounting software: also referred to as *online accounting software,* is accounting software that is hosted on remote servers and accessed via the internet. Data is sent into "the cloud", where it is processed and returned to the user. This means you can connect to your accounting software from any internet-capable device such as your laptop, i-pad or smartphone. See *cloud.*

cloud computing: storing and accessing data and programs over the internet instead of your computer's hard drive. Using the cloud frees the business from having to install and update software on individual desktop computers. See *cloud.*

closing balance: is the amount remaining in an account, positive or negative, at the end of an accounting period or year end.

coding: a term used to describe the allocation of a transaction amount to an account in the chart of accounts.

coffice: a combination of coffee shop and office. A coffice is a coffee shop used as an office, usually by using an internet connection with your laptop computer.

collateral: is property or assets made available by a borrower as security against a loan. Collateral is sometimes called security. See *security.*

columnar ledger accounts: are used in accounting software with debit and credit columns for recording entries and another column that shows the balance of the account after each entry is posted. See *ledger account, T account.*

company: a company is an entity that has a separate legal existence from its owners. The owners of the company are known as members or shareholders. Its legal status gives a company the same rights as a natural person which means that a company can incur debt, sue and be sued. Companies are managed by company officers who are called directors and company secretaries.

Small business owners often use a private company structure called a proprietary limited company (which has the words 'Pty Ltd' after the name). This type of company does not sell its shares to the public and has limited liability. Large companies that sell shares to the public can still limit their liability and will often have the abbreviation 'Ltd' after their name.

company director: a person appointed to take responsibility for the policy formation and control of a company. In small companies, company directors are usually involved in the management of the company. Company directors' have many responsibilities and are governed by Corporations Law.

company secretary: the person responsible for ensuring compliance with statutory and regulatory requirements and that the decisions of the board of directors are implemented. Despite the name, the role is not clerical or secretarial.

compilation: financial statements that have not been audited so the accountant is unable to express an opinion or any other form of assurance on them. Compiled financial statements provide business owners with a basic inspection of an organisation's data and are useful when preparing tax returns and analysing financial results.

compound interest: is interest calculated on principal plus interest earned in previous periods.

computer network: is a digital telecommunications network which allows a group of two or more computing devices to exchange data with each other through connections established over cable media such as wires or optic cables, or wireless media such as Wi-Fi. See *internet.*

computerised accounting: is an accounting system that uses an accounting software, for recording financial transactions electronically. Accounting software processes data and creates reports much faster than manual systems. Calculations are done automatically in software programs, minimising errors and increasing efficiency. See *manual accounting.*

consolidated financial statements: combined financial statements of a *parent company* and one or *more of its subsidiaries.* Thus the report combines the assets, liabilities, revenues and expenses of any companies that it owns. See *parent company.*

consumer confidence: the degree of optimism that consumers feel about the overall state of the economy and their personal financial situation. When consumer confidence is high, consumers make more purchases. When confidence is low, consumers tend to save more and spend less. Consumer confidence is a key indicator for the overall shape of the economy.

contingent liabilities: possible financial obligations that a company needs to report when it determines that an event is likely to happen.

contra: if a payment is made into an account, and then that same payment is paid out of the account for a reason, it is called a *contra* – the two figures contra or cancel each other out of the account. For example: $100 was paid *into* the rent account. The owner realised that he should have used a different account so he pays the $100 *out* of the rent account. This is the contra.

control accounts: a general ledger account containing only *summary amounts.* The details for each control account will be found in a related (but separate) subsidiary ledger.

Common examples include: The *accounts receivable (debtors) control account,* in the general ledger reflects the total of the individual debtor's balances in the subsidiary ledger. The *accounts payable (creditors) control account,* in the general ledger reflects the total of the individual creditor's balances in the subsidiary ledger. Control accounts are created to remove unnecessary detail from the general ledger. See **subsidiary ledger.**

conversion balances: when a business transfers their bookkeeping records from one accounting software program to another they are 'converting' their books. The closing balances from the old software is entered into the new software as opening balances. These balances are called *conversion balances.*

cook the books: fraudulent accounting practices used by corporations to make their financial statements, particularly profits, look better than they are. See **financial statements, profit.**

cost of goods sold (COGS): refers to the *direct costs* attributable to the goods sold in a company. This amount includes the cost of the *raw materials* used in creating the goods, along with *direct labour* costs used to produce the goods.

<u>Formula for Cost of Goods Sold (COGS):</u>

Beginning Inventory
plus Purchases
<u>less Ending Inventory</u>

Cost of Goods Sold

The beginning inventory for the year is the inventory left over from the previous year. Any additional productions or purchases made are added to the beginning inventory. At the end of the year the products not sold are subtracted from the beginning inventory and additional purchases. This is the *cost of goods sold* for the year. Cost of goods sold is also known as **cost of sales.**

credit: in accounting there two meanings of the term credit:

i) In double entry accounting any transaction that increases liabilities, equity or revenue/income or that decreases assets or expenses. Credits are found on the *right-hand side* of the ledger account in *double entry accounting*.

ii) Receiving something of value now and promising to pay for it later, often with a finance charge added by the lender. Credit can include loans, credit and store cards, hire purchases, supplier credit. When you open an account with a supplier you would most likely fill in a form called a *credit application*.

credit card: credit cards enable individuals or businesses to pay for goods and services using the money of the credit card provider, up to a set limit. The money is paid back to the credit card provider, along with any monthly interest charge, in regular monthly instalments or in full with one repayment.

credit note: a document that provides a refund to a customer for goods returned or sold at the wrong price. A credit note is also called an ***adjustment note.***

credit policy: a set of rules that sets out the terms for any customer who receives credit from the business. See ***credit terms.***

credit report: documents your financial and personal information as collected by credit reporting agencies and used to calculate your *credit score*. See ***credit score.***

credit risk: is the risk of default on a debt that may arise from a borrower failing to repay a loan or make the required repayments.

credit score: is an numerical score that appears in your credit report, that lenders look at to work out if they should lend you money or give you credit. The credit score sums up the information on your credit report into one number. If you have a high score, you have demonstrated a history of financial responsibility and are considered a lesser credit risk than someone with a lower score. A credit score is sometimes referred to as *credit rating*. See ***credit report.***

credit terms: the terms which indicate when payment is due for sales made to customers on credit. For example, the credit terms might be 5/10, net 30. This means the amount is due in 30 days, however, if the amount is paid in 10 days a discount of 5% will be applied. Credit terms are also called *terms of credit.*

credit transaction: a transaction where *no money changes hands at the time the transaction* occurs. Here the business allows the customer to purchase goods or receive services, on credit and thus pay for them later. See *cash transaction.*

creditors: the person or business to whom your business *owes* money for purchases made. They're also referred to as *trade creditors, payables or accounts payable.* See *accounts payable.*

creditors ledger: See *accounts payable ledger.*

crm: a customer relationship management (crm) system provides a central place where businesses can store customer information, track customer interactions and share this information with staff. It allows businesses to manage relationships with customers, helping the business to grow.

cryptocurrency: is a digital or virtual currency that uses cryptography for security. A cryptocurrency is difficult to counterfeit because of this security feature. See *bitcoin.*

csv file: comma **s**eparated **v**alues file. Files in this format (.csv) are used to exchange data between different applications. All csv files are plain text, can contain numbers and letters only and structure data in tabular or table form. Microsoft Excel is most commonly used program for csv files. See *import (data), export (data).*

current asset: anything that a business owns that can realistically be converted into cash within the next twelve months. Examples of such assets include: cash in bank accounts and petty cash, money owed to the business (accounts receivable) by its customers, short-term investments such as a term deposit that matures within a year, inventory – items in stock that you buy and sell.

current liability: an amount owed by the business which is due to be paid within the next twelve months. Examples of current liabilities include credit cards, overdrafts, the money the business owes to suppliers (accounts payable), customer deposits, employee wages.

current ratio: a measure of liquidity. It measures the proportion of current assets available to offset current liabilities. The current ratio is calculated by dividing current assets by current liabilities:

$$\text{Current Ratio} = \frac{\text{Current Assets}}{\text{Current Liabilities}}$$

A ratio above 1 means current assets exceed liabilities, and generally, the higher the ratio, the better. The current ratio is also referred to as the ***acid test ratio, liquidity ratio, quick ratio or working capital ratio.*** See ***liquidity, working capital.***

customer: is the recipient of a *good or service,* obtained from a seller via a financial transaction. A customer is also known as a client, buyer or purchaser.

cyberattack: is a malicious attempt by an individual or organisation to breach the information system of another individual or organisation. They are usually aimed at accessing, changing or destroying sensitive information, extorting money from users, or interrupting normal business processes. See ***ransomware, backup.***

cybersecurity: the technologies, processes and practices designed to protect networks, devices, programs and data from attack, damage or unauthorised access. See ***cyberattack.***

CHAPTER 4

TERMS

dashboard: the area in online accounting software that provides at a *quick overview and an insight* to how the business is performing, further dashboards then provide details on other areas of the business.

data: numbers, facts, statistics, the financial information entered and found inside the accounting system.

database: is an organised collection of data, generally stored and accessed electronically form a computer system.

debit: any transaction that increases assets or expenses, or that decreases liabilities, equity or revenue/income. A debit balance is found on the *left-hand side* of the ledger account in *double entry accounting*.

debit cards: deduct money directly from your bank account compared to a credit card which gives you access to a line of debt issued by a bank.

debt: is the money owed by the borrower or debtor, to a lender or creditor.

debtor: a person, a business or an organisation that owes your business money. See ***accounts receivable.***

debtors ledger: See ***accounts receivable ledger.***

deductible expense: is an expense that income tax law allows you to subtract from your taxable gross income. Deductible expenses reduce your tax liability. See ***non-deductible expense.***

default super fund: is the superannuation fund into which an employer will make employee super contributions if the employee does not nominate a fund of their own choosing. A default super fund is also referred to as an employer-nominated fund. (Australia only). See ***super guarantee.***

deferred payment: an agreement between the lender and borrower allowing the borrower to take possession of goods immediately with a commitment to start making payments at a future date, usually by instalments.

deflation: is a general decline in prices for goods and services, typically associated with a contraction in the supply of money and credit in the economy. During deflation, the purchasing power of currency rises over time.

delivery docket: a vendor may provide a delivery docket with the items being shipped, posted or delivered. These will often have a description of items being delivered so the buyer can check it against their order immediately upon its arrival.

deposit: money (cash, EFPOS, cheques) paid into a bank account.

deposit slip: the paper record that accompanies the cash or cheques deposit. It details what bank account the funds are being paid into, the date, details and amount of the deposit.

depreciation: the accounting practice where the cost of a tangible asset is reduced by a certain percentage each year to show that the asset is being used up (aging). The percentage used is based on the effective life of the asset, usually as determined by the tax office. See *effective life of an asset, prime cost depreciation, diminishing value.*

depreciation schedule: a report showing the fixed assets that a business owns, the cost value of each asset, and how much depreciation has been claimed so far for each one.

description: is the section in data entry of a financial transaction that describes the item or service purchased or sold.

desktop: either i) a computer suitable for use at an ordinary desk or ii) the working area of a computer screen that contains icons (small symbols or pictures) representing files, programs and other features of the computer. See *laptop.*

desktop sharing: See *screen sharing.*

digital: showing information in the form of an electronic image.

digital copy: a scanned or electronic copy of a document that can be stored on your computer, mobile device or online.

digital download: See *downloading.*

digital signature: guarantees the authenticity of an electronic document or message in digital communication and uses encryption techniques to provide proof of original and unmodified documentation. Digital signatures are used in e-commerce, in regulatory filings and other situations that rely on forgery or tampering detection techniques. A digital signature is different from an electronic signature which is often associated with contracts where there is intention to sign the document or contract by the party involved. See **electronic signature.**

digitalisation: the result of using digitisation to improve the business processes.

digitisation: is the process of converting information from a physical format into a digital format that can be understood by computer systems or other electronic devices. The term is used when converting information, like text, images or voices and sounds, into binary code. For example: in business, digitisation can be the conversion of paper documents into digital copy.

diminishing value: a depreciation method where you calculate depreciation on the written down value of the asset. This method assumes that the value of a depreciating asset decreases more in the early years of its effective life. See *depreciation*.

direct costs: are expenses that can be directly traced to a product. See *cost of goods sold.*

direct data entry: is an online process in which data is entered into a system and written into its online files. The data may be entered by an operator at a keyboard or by a data capture device. See *entered.*

director: See *company director.*

discontinued operations: business activities that a company halts, such as the closing of a factory or the sale of a division within a company.

discount: a reduction from the full amount of a price.

dividends: are the portion of a company's profits that are paid out to shareholders according to the number of shares that the shareholder holds.

docket: a document that contains information about a product sold from one business to another, such as a delivery docket.

document management and data extraction software: enables documents that are *auto-fetched, emailed* or paper documents *scanned* and *uploaded directly* into the document management system to be automatically filed in an electronic filing cabinet or file. Data is automatically extracted from the document which is then ready to be reviewed and 'published' to your online accounting software along with a digital copy of the document. See ***paperless office.***

document management software: enables electronic files or filing cabinets your business can use for filing all digital and scanned paper documents. Any paper copies of documents can be uploaded directly into the document management system with a scanner. See ***paperless office.***

double-entry accounting: also referred to as *double-entry bookkeeping*, is an accounting method that requires a company to record every transaction using debits and credits to show both sides of the transaction. All transactions affect at *least* two accounts and *all the debits need to equal the same as the credits.*

A *debit* is any transaction that increases assets or expenses, or that decreases liabilities, equity or revenue/income. A debit balance is found on the *left-hand side* of the ledger account in *double entry accounting.*

A *credit* is any transaction that increases liabilities, equity or revenue/income or that decreases assets or expenses. Credits are found on the *right-hand side* of the ledger account in *double entry accounting.*

The following table summarises how, for each account type (account classification), a debit or credit affects the accounts:

Debit (DR)/Credit (CR) table:

Debit (DR)	Account Type	Credit (CR)
Increases	ASSETS	Decreases
Increases	EXPENSES	Decreases
Decreases	LIABILITIES	Increases
Decreases	EQUITY	Increases
Decreases	REVENUE/INCOME	Increases

For example:

1. You buy a motor vehicle for $1,000 Cash

(no GST/sales tax in this example)

Using the above Debit (DR)/Credit (CR) table:

Motor Vehicle	Asset	Increases DR	$1,000
Bank	Asset	Decreases CR	$1,000

The motor vehicle purchase has increased assets, hence a debit (DR) and as cash has been used to pay for the motor vehicle, the bank asset has decreased, hence a credit (CR).

The journal entry is:

DR	Motor vehicle account	$1,000	
CR	Bank account		$1,000

For example:

2. You buy a car for $1,000 with a loan.

(no GST/sales tax in this example)

D Terms

Using the above Debit (DR)/Credit (CR) table:

Motor Vehicle	Asset	Increases DR	$1,000
Loan Payable	Liabilities	Increases CR	$1,000

The motor vehicle purchase has increased assets, hence a debit (DR) and as a loan has been incurred to pay for the motor vehicle, the liabilities have increased, hence a credit (CR).

The journal entry is:

DR	Motor vehicle account	$1,000	
CR	Loan Payable account		$1,000

Learning debits, credits and the accounts the transaction relates to takes practice. See *journal entry.*

downloading: is when a file, whether that be a document, software, video, music, or some other data, is copied from a *device* or *the internet* to your computer or other device. Downloading a file makes a copy of that file on whatever device you are using.

drag and drop: the user selects a virtual object by "grabbing it" (with pointing device) and dragging it to a different location or onto another virtual object.

drawee: in relation to cheques, is the place (bank) where the cheque is drawn out of.

drawer: is the person who writes the cheque. The drawer completes details on the cheque such as the date, amount payable, payee, signs it, thus ordering their bank, known as the *drawee*, to pay the payee the amount of money stated. See **refer to drawer, bounce, payee, cheque, drawee.**

drawings: funds withdrawn from a business by the business owner for their personal use or personal spending by the business owner paid for out of business funds. Drawings are also referred to as ***owners' drawings.***

drill down: in online accounting software is a capability that allows the user to drill down from a summary view of the data, by *clicking on the hyperlinks* provided to expose more detailed information.

drop-down menu: is a list of items that appear when clicking on a button or text selection in the menu. For example, many programs have a 'File' drop-down menu on the top left of their screen. Clicking on the 'File' text shows the drop-down menu with additional options. See *menu bar.*

CHAPTER 5

TERMS

earnings per share (EPS): is the *amount of net income* that a company makes *per share of stock* available on the *market*. It is important in determining a share's price and is also used to calculate the price-to-earnings (P/E) valuation ratio, where E in P/E refers to EPS. EPP is calculated as follows:

$$EPS = \frac{\text{Net Income}}{\text{average shares outstanding}}$$

See *shares outstanding, price-to-earnings*.

e-banking: also referred to as *electronic banking*. See *online banking*.

e-billing: also referred to as *electronic billing* or *electronic bill payment and presentment,* is when a seller such as individual, company or other organisation sends its bills or invoices over the internet and customers have the option to pay the bills electronically. See *invoice, e-mail*.

e-business: also referred to as *electronic business,* is the conduct of business processes on the internet. E-commerce is a part of e-business. See *e-commerce*.

e-commerce: also referred to as *electronic commerce,* is the buying and selling of goods or services using the internet, and the transfer of money and data to execute these transactions.

e-mail: also referred to as *electronic mail or email,* describes messages sent electronically from one computer user to one or more recipients via a network.

e-signature: See *electronic signature.*

economic cycle: is the downward and upward movement of gross domestic product (GDP) around its long-term growth trend. The length of an economic cycle is the period of time containing a single boom and contraction sequence. These fluctuations involve shifts over time between periods of relatively rapid economic growth (expansions or booms) and periods of relative stagnation or decline (contractions or recessions). An economic cycle is also referred to as a *business cycle* or *trade cycle.* See *gross domestic product (GDP), boom, recession*.

economic recession: See *recession.*

economy: is the state of a country or region, is all activities in terms of the production and consumption of goods and services and the supply of money.

effective life of an asset: the period of time a business asset is expected to be useful to produce income. It is used to work out the asset's decline in value (or depreciation) for an income tax deduction. The effective life of an asset is usually determined by the tax office. The effective life of an asset is also referred to as the *assets useful life.* See *depreciation.*

electronic funds transfer (EFT): is a transaction that takes place over a computerised network, either among accounts at the same bank or to different accounts at separate financial institutions. EFTs include direct-debit transactions, direct deposits, ATM withdrawals and online bill pay services.

electronic funds transfer at point of sale (EFTPOS): is an electronic payment system for goods and services, involving electronic funds transfers from a customer's bank account to a merchant (business) bank account using an EFTPOS machine at the point of sale. To pay by EFTPOS a customer needs a payment card such as a debit or credit card.

electronic lodgement: using the internet site of an organization to lodge a document electronically instead of sending it as a paper document by post.

electronic signature: sometimes referred to as an **e-signature**, can be verbal, a simple click of the box or any electronically signed authorisation that is associated with a document or contract where there *is intention to sign the document or contract* by the party involved. They are legally binding once all parties have shown their commitment and intent to enter into the contract. An electronic signature is different from a digital signature, which is mainly used to secure documents and is authorized by certification authorities. See *digital signature.*

embezzlement: theft or misappropriation of funds placed in one's trust or belonging to one's employer.

engagement letter: is a written agreement that describes the business relationship and expectations between the client and the business. The letter contains details of the scope of the work to be done, its terms and costs.

entered: once the details of a financial transaction have been recorded into the ledger accounts, the transaction is said to be *entered*. A transaction entered into the ledger is also referred to as ***posted,*** or ***recorded***. See ***direct data entry.***

entity: refers to a type or structure of business such as individual, company, partnership, association, club or cooperative, that has created or formed to carry on a business.

entrepreneur: a person who takes on the risks of starting a new business.

entries: all financial transactions input to the accounting system are called ***entries.***

equity: See ***shareholders equity.***

equity capital: the amount of capital (funds) contributed to the company by the business owners or shareholders.

expense: is the money spent, or costs incurred, by a business to generate revenues. For example: costs such as advertising, bank charges, rent, phone and internet are classified as an expense. Expenses are shown in the profit and loss report. See ***deductible expense, non-deductible expense***.

export (data): most accounting software programs allow the export of information to excel or pdf for various uses. Creditor payments can be exported from the software and uploaded directly to the bank for payment so that the account and other details do not have to be manually entered before payment. See **csv file, aba file.**

export (goods): items or goods that can be shipped outside a country either by land, sea or air.

extraordinary item: an event or transaction that is considered abnormal, not related to ordinary company activities, and unlikely to recur in the foreseeable future. For example: gains or losses from a lawsuit, losses from catastrophic events, such as earthquakes, tsunamis. Extraordinary items are shown separately from the annual profit and loss calculation and are explained further in the notes to the financial statements.

CHAPTER 6

TERMS

fair market value (FMV): is an *estimate of* the market value of an asset, based on what a willing buyer would probably pay a willing seller, when neither party is under any pressure to buy or sell and both knowledgeable about the asset.

fair work commission: See *the fair work commission (FWC)*

fair work ombudsman: See *the fair work ombudsman (FWO)*

fiduciary: is a person or organisation that acts on behalf of another person or persons to manage assets. A fiduciary owes to that other entity the duties of good faith, trust and is ethically bound to act in the other's best interests. See *trusts.*

file: the physical or digital place in which a business puts all its documents in a specialised method. It can also refer to the business's accounting data contained within your accounting software.

filed: taxpayers meeting statutory requirements must send various returns on time to a government department, using the prescribed forms, for example "I have *filed* my tax return". Filed can also refer to putting away documents in a systematic method.

finance lease: a lease which effectively transfers from the lessor (owner) to the lessee the bulk of the risks and benefits that go with ownership of the leased property. See *operating lease.*

financial asset: is a non-physical asset whose value is derived from a contractual right to receive cash, as in bank deposits, bonds, or evidence of an ownership in an entity, as in stocks and shares.

financial statements: are the business reports of its financial transactions over various periods, such as monthly, quarterly or annually. The three key statements are the balance sheet, income statement and statement of cash flows. Financial statements are also referred to as the *reports*, *accounts*, or *annual accounts*. See *notes to the financial statements, annual report.*

financial transactions: is an event that changes the monetary value of an asset, liability or owner's equity of a business. The four main types of financial transactions are sales, purchases, receipts and payments. These are recorded in the *special journals*: sales journal, purchases journal, cash receipts journal and cash payments journal. See ***special journals.***

finished goods: are goods that have completed the manufacturing process, but which have not yet been sold to customers.

first in, first out (FIFO): a system of valuing inventory in which it is assumed that goods are used in the same sequence in which they were bought - the first items you bring into inventory are the first ones you sell. The goods on hand represent those last purchased and are valued at the latest purchase price. See ***last in, first out (LIFO).***

fiscal year: is an accounting year that, unlike a calendar year, doesn't necessarily end on 31 December. A *fiscal year* is a twelve month period used for accounting purposes. For example, a company might operate on a fiscal year that begins on 1 July and ends on 30 June. See ***calendar year.***

fixed assets: are non-current assets that a company uses in its production of goods and services that have a life of more than one year. They are recorded on the balance sheet and listed as property, plant and equipment. Fixed assets are also referred to as tangible assets, meaning they can be physically touched. See ***non-current asset.***

fixed costs: expenses that stay *constant* whatever the amount of goods or services produced by the business. Examples include: interest or monthly rent paid. Fixed costs are also referred to as ***overhead costs, overheads*** or ***indirect costs.*** See ***variable costs.***

fixed deposit: See ***term deposit.***

fixture: attachment to real property that is not intended to be moved and would create damage to the property if it were moved.

foreign exchange gains and losses: occur when a transaction is made to purchase or sell goods and services in a foreign currency. The date at which the transaction is made will have a different exchange rate to the date of payment or receipt because exchange rates fluctuate constantly. These different exchange rates cause financial gains or losses that need to be identified in the accounts.

Foreign exchange gains occur when the business is required to pay less to the supplier or receives more than the original conversion amount.

Foreign exchange losses occur when the business is required to pay more to the supplier or receives less than the original conversion amount.

forex: abbrev for foreign exchange.

formation expenses: expenses incurred in setting up a new company, such as registration of a new company name.

franked dividends: company profits paid to shareholders which that *have tax credits* attached to the dividend. See ***imputation credit, unfranked dividend.***

fraudulent financial reporting: a deliberate attempt by a business to distort its financial statements to make its financial results look better than they are.

freight in: transportation charges on merchandise purchased for resale.

freight out: transportation charges on merchandise sold.

fringe benefit: are forms of compensation that employers provide to employees outside of a stated wage or salary. Common examples of fringe benefits include use of a company car, medical and dental insurance.

fringe benefit tax (FBT): is a tax employers pay on certain fringe benefits they provide to their employees, including their employees' family or other associates.

full disclosure: requirement to disclose all material facts relevant to a transaction.

funds: all the financial resources of a firm, such as cash in hand, bank balance, accounts receivable. Funds can also refer to a sum of money made available for a certain purpose.

CHAPTER 7

TERMS

general journal: records all the transactions except for the ones which are recorded in a *special journal* such as a sales journal, purchases journal etc. It states the date of the transaction, description, credit and debit information in a double entry accounting system. See ***special journals.***

general ledger: this is the *main ledger* for a business. Each section of this ledger represents one account found in the chart of accounts. The details from every business transaction, such as the date, description and amount are posted into the appropriate general ledger account. The accounts are arranged in the general ledger (and the chart of accounts) with the balance sheet accounts appearing first followed by the income statement accounts. See ***account, ledger, 'T' account, columnar account.***

general purpose financial report (GPFR): are financial statements prepared in accordance with all Australian Accounting Standards. An entity defined as a *reporting entity* is required to prepare GRFR. See ***reporting entity.***

generally accepted accounting principles (GAAP): rules for financial reporting that dictate that a business's financial reporting is relevant, reliable, consistent and presented in a way that allows the report reader to compare the results to prior years.

going-concern: is the assumption that an entity will remain in business for the foreseeable future.

goods and services tax (GST): is a broad-based tax of 10% on *most goods, services and other items sold or consumed* in Australia. Generally, businesses and other organisations registered for GST will include GST in the price they charge for their goods and services and claim credits for the GST included in the price of goods and services they buy for their business.

goodwill account: an account that appears on the balance sheet when a business has been brought for more than the actual value of its assets minus its liabilities. Goodwill include things such as customer loyalty. See ***intangible assets.***

gross domestic product (GDP): is the total monetary or market values of all the finished goods and services produced within a county during a specific time period. It reflects the country's economic health. See *economic cycle*.

gross margin (GM): is a percentage calculated by taking gross profit and dividing by revenue for the same period. It represents the profitability of a company after deducting the Cost of Goods Sold.

$$Gross\ Margin\ Percentage = \frac{Gross\ Profit}{Revenue} \times 100$$

gross profit (GP): indicates the profitability of a company in dollars, without taking overhead expenses into account. It is calculated by subtracting the Cost of Goods Sold from Revenue for the same period:

Gross Profit = Revenue − Cost of Goods Sold

If the cost of goods sold is more than the revenue a *gross loss* results.

CHAPTER 8

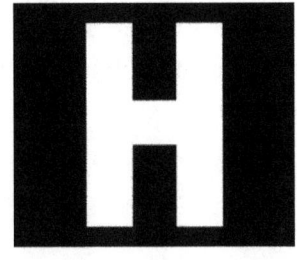

TERMS

hard copy: is a *printed* digital document file on paper, whereas *soft copy* is an unprinted *electronic* document file that exists in any digital form on computers, mobile devices etc.

header accounts: The headings under which detail accounts or sub-accounts are grouped in the chart of accounts.

hire purchase: is an arrangement whereby a customer agrees to a contract to acquire assets, by paying an initial instalment and repays the balance of the price of the asset plus interest over a specified period. The ownership is not officially transferred to the buyer until all the payments have been made.

historical cost: is the original cost of an asset to an entity.

holding company: is a company that *exists to own subsidiaries* and does not have its own operating business ventures. It is one type of parent company. See ***parent company.***

CHAPTER 9

TERMS

icon: a small picture or symbol on a computer screen that you point to and click on to give the computer an instruction. For example: the printer icon to print documents.

impaired asset: is an asset that has a market price less than the value listed on the balance sheet. These assets are often written down to reflect the current market value. See *write down.*

import (data): is data brought into the accounting records through a digital import. This could include bank transactions which can be downloaded from the bank in a format such as csv, or it could be contact names and addresses from a database program or other applications. See *csv file.*

import (goods): goods that are purchased from other countries for use in one's own country. Visible imports are items such as clothing, cars and wine; invisible imports are such things as freight payments, dividend payments and royalties.

imputation credit: a tax credit that is part of a franked dividend. See *franked dividend.*

in arrears: an amount not paid at the time originally agreed to and is overdue.

income: See *revenue.*

income statement: See *profit and loss statement, statement of financial performance.*

income tax: tax levied directly on business and personal income. See *tax.*

incorporation: the process of forming a company. Incorporation is carried out by lodging the necessary documents – memorandum and articles of association, notice of registered office, list of directors with ASIC and paying the required fees. The date shown on the certificate of incorporation is the date from which the company exists with corporate status. (Australia).

indirect costs: See *fixed costs.*

industry superannuation fund: a superannuation fund covering several employers, usually within one industry or sector.

inflation: is the rate at which the prices for goods and services is rising and consequently, the purchasing power of money is falling.

initial public offering (IPO): when a private company goes public for the first time, it offers its shares to the public.

input tax credit: the credit a business claims for the GST paid on goods or services.

inside information: corporate affairs that have not yet been made public.

insider trading: an illegal practice of trading on the stock exchange to one's own advantage through having access to confidential or inside information about a company.

insolvent: the state of being unable to pay the money owed, when the debt is due for payment. A company or an individual can be insolvent.

instalment activity statement (IAS): a form used to report for monthly PAYG withholding tax if GST is paid quarterly, or a form used to pay PAYG withholding tax and PAYG instalment tax for businesses that aren't registered for GST (Australia only).

instalment payments: the regular payments to be made on a borrowing such as hire purchase, personal loan, mortgage. The payments normally include a substantial interest component, especially early in the loan. See ***credit, hire purchase.***

insurance: protection against possible event. You can buy insurance against an event which might or might not happen, such as burglary, an illness, loss of income, loss of property, accidents, natural disasters, a legal liability etc. Any form of insurance entails the payment of a sum (premium) to the insurer and this is often split into regular instalments.

intangible assets: are assets which are not physical in nature but have a value such as a goodwill, patents, brand recognition, trade secrets.

intellectual property: works, products, or marketing identities for which a company owns the exclusive rights, such as copyrights, patents, and trademarks.

interest expenses: charges that must be paid on borrowed money, usually a percentage of the debt.

interim financial statements: financial statements that report on the operations of a business for less than one year. Interim financial statements are also referred to as *interim reports.*

internal controls: procedures in place that safeguard the flow of money into and out of the business.

internal financial report: a summary of a company's financial results that's distributed within the company only.

internet: a means of connecting a computer to another computer anywhere in the world via dedicated routers and servers. When two computers are connected over the internet, they can send and receive all kinds of information such as text, graphics, voice, video, and computer programs. Other names for the internet include: *the net, the web, world wide web (www), the cloud, hyperspace, cyberspace, information server, information highway, information superhighway, online, online network.*

internet banking: See *online banking.*

inventory: refers to the value of *stocks,* as distinct from fixed assets. An inventory would include a list of items which are held for sale in the ordinary course of business or which are in the process of production for the purpose of sale, or which are to be used in the production of goods or services which will be for sale. See *stock, periodic method, perpetual method.*

inventory turnover ratio: shows how many times a company has sold and replaced inventory during a given period. Calculating inventory turnover can help businesses make better decisions on pricing, manufacturing, marketing and purchasing new inventory. Inventory turnover ratio can be calculated as:

$$Inventory\ Turnover = \frac{Sales}{Average\ Inventory}$$

where: Average Inventory = (Beginning Inventory – Ending Inventory) ÷ 2

investor: one who lays out money, usually by lending or purchasing, in the expectation of profiting from interest earnings or capital gain.

invoice: a document that details the *purchase or sale* of goods or services. The invoice will show the transaction details such as date, invoice number, quantity, description, cost, total, payment terms. When a business *purchases* goods or services it will receive a *purchase invoice* and when the business *sells* goods or services it will provide a *sales invoice* to the customer. See ***tax invoice.***

invoicing: preparing invoices to charge customers for goods or services they have purchased from the business. See ***billing.***

involuntary administration: occurs when it is not the company that decides to go into *administration*, but the creditors. This usually happens after a company has failed to repay its debts. It aims to help the company repay debts in order to escape liquidation (if possible). See ***voluntary administration.***

involuntary bankruptcy: see ***bankruptcy.***

issued shares: are the shares of the company that are issued by the company and held by its shareholder.

CHAPTER 10

TERMS

joint venture: a business arrangement between two or more parties, to use or pool their expertise to complete a specific project.

jointly and severally liable: in a partnership, a creditor may sue any one of the partners for repayment of a partnership debt. If one partner pays the debt, then that partner may pursue other partners to collect their share of the debt obligation.

journal: a list of transactions, usually sorted by date.

journal entry: an adjusting entry which debits and credits selected accounts. The journal describes which account is being debited and which account is being credited, the date, the reason for the journal and a reference. See *general journal, special journals.*

just in time: a method to have materials delivered by suppliers just as the materials are needed, to eliminate the need for the buyer to store inventories of component parts.

CHAPTER 11

TERMS

k: a symbol that represents 1000. For example: 1K means 1,000, 2K means 2,000.

key performance indictor (KPI): is a measurable value that demonstrates how effectively a company is achieving key business objectives. Organisations use KPIs to evaluate their success at reaching targets. For example: a typical KPI in most organisations is the sales budget that specifies what revenue each sales representative is expected to achieve during a given period.

CHAPTER 12

TERMS

labour: physical or mental effort, work

laptop: is a personal computer designed for portability. A laptop has an all-in-one design, with a built-in monitor, keyboard, touchpad (which replaces the mouse) and speakers. It is also quicker to set up and there are fewer cables to get in the way. See ***desktop, PC, PC or Mac.***

last in, first out (LIFO): a system of valuing inventory on the basis that the latest items purchased are the first to be used in production or sales. Goods on hand represent earliest purchases and are valued at the earlier prices. See ***first in, first out (FIFO).***

lease: an agreement between two parties under which one is granted the right to use the property of the other for a specified period in return for a series of payments by the user to the owner.

ledger: all the accounts, showing all the detail of all transactions in each account for a particular period of time. In computerised accounting the ledger will consist of a computer report. Traditionally, in a manual accounting system, a ledger was a book with separate pages for each account. See ***general ledger, subsidiary ledger***

ledger account: See ***account.***

legal entity: may be an individual, company, or organisation that has legal rights and obligations such as the legal capacity to enter into contracts, to sue, and to be sued.

lessee: the person/entity to whom a lease is granted and who pays the due instalments (rent) to the lessor.

lessor: the grantor of the lease, who remains the owner of the leased property throughout the term of the lease and who receives lease payments from the lessee.

liability: any kind of debts that the business owes, such as credit card debts, supplier accounts, overdrafts, bank loans, mortgages, money owing to the tax office.

lien: the right to hold property of another person as security until a debt owed by that person has been paid. For example a mechanic may have a lien over a car until the business is paid for the work done.

limited liability: a legal concept which protects shareholders in a company by *restricting their liabilities* to the value of their shares, even if the company has debts exceeding that value.

listed company: a company whose shares are quoted on the stock exchange and are available to be bought and sold by the public.

liquid assets: assets which can be turned into cash easily or swiftly with minimum capital loss. See *liquidity.*

liquidation: the winding up of a business by its members or its creditors. The assets are sold, liabilities settled as far as possible and any remaining cash returned to shareholders.

liquidator: a person appointed to oversee the winding up and liquidation of a company.

liquidity: refers to how easily assets can be converted into cash. Assets like shares and bonds are very liquid since they can be easily converted into cash.

liquidity ratio: See *current ratio.*

loan: is the lending of money by individuals, or entities to other individuals or entities. The recipient incurs a debt, and is usually liable to pay interest on the debt until it is repaid.

lodge: present the relevant document formally to the proper authority.

long-term assets: holdings that a company will use for more than a twelve month period, such as buildings, land and equipment.

long-term debt or liabilities: financial obligations that a company must pay more than twelve months into the future, such as mortgages on buildings.

luxury car tax (LCT): is a tax on cars with a GST-inclusive value above the luxury car tax threshold. It is currently payable at the rate of 33% on the portion the GST-inclusive value which exceeds the luxury car tax threshold. The threshold is set by the Australian Tax Office for each financial year.

CHAPTER 13

TERMS

majority interest: the position a company has when it owns more than 50 percent of another company's shares.

manual accounting: is a system of accounting where the records are maintained by hand, without using accounting software. Instead transactions are written in journals, account books and physical registers. The information is manually collated into a set of financial statements.

mark-up: is the difference between the sales price of a good or service and cost. A mark-up is *added into the total cost* incurred in order to cover the costs of doing business and make a profit. Mark-up can be expressed as a percentage of the total cost or set as a fixed amount. For example: if the original cost is $4.00 and the mark-up is 25%, the sales price should be $4.00 + $4.00*25/100 = $5.00.

market share: percentage of industry sales of a particular company or product.

market value: the amount you would receive for an asset were you to offer it for sale.

matching principle: combines *accrual accounting* (where revenues and expenses are recorded as they are incurred, no matter when cash is received) with the *revenue recognition principle* (which states that revenues should be recognised *when they are earned* or *realized*, no matter when cash is received). The matching principle is not used in *cash accounting* (where revenues and expenses are only recorded when cash changes hands.)

material: information is material if its omission or misstatement could influence the economic decisions of users taken on the basis of those statements. For example: A company omits the existence of a lawsuit form its financial statements disclosures that indicates the potential for a large settlement that could bankrupt it, is material to the financial statements.

material changes: changes that may have a significant financial impact on a company's earnings. **material misstatement:** an error that significantly impacts a company's financial position. See *material.*

meeting: a gathering of two or more people at which something is discussed or a formal agenda is followed.

menu bar: within accounting software is a thin, horizontal bar of menu item titles that, when clicked, display a *drop-down menu* of other items. It provides the user with a standard place to find the majority of a program's essential functions. See ***drop-down menu, toolbars, navigation bar.***

merchandise: goods that have been purchased in completed form, which will then be sold to the public or other businesses.

micro-business: a small business that typically *employ between one and four people*. Micro businesses are often owned and operated by a self–employed individual with no employees.

minutes: written details of a meeting, usually certified by the chairman as being an accurate record of the proceedings.

monetise: convert to money.

money laundering: is 'washing' money from criminal activity that is considered dirty, by channeling it through a 'respectable' institution or transaction to make it look clean, as if it has come from a legitimate source. Money laundering is also a crime.

month end: at the end of the month, there are various accounting procedures required to close of the month such as: reconciling the bank account to the last day of the month, ensuring all sales have been invoiced to customers, checking that all supplier invoices dated to the last day of the month have been entered into the accounting system, reviewing the general ledger accounts to ensure information has been coded to the right place. Reconciling of other relevant items. Once this is completed the month should be 'closed off' (or locked) so no new data can be entered back into that month. These procedures ensure that your data is accurate for preparing the financial statements.

mortgage: is a loan where property is used as security. The borrower agrees to make payments over a set period of time until the lender is repaid in full. See ***security.***

myGov: is a service provided by the Australian government to access a range of government services online.

CHAPTER 14

TERMS

national employment standards (NES): are 10 minimum terms and conditions of employment that apply to national workplace relations system employees.

The 10 NES relate to the following matters: Maximum weekly hours; Requests for flexible working arrangements; Parental leave and related entitlements; Annual leave; Personal/carer's leave, compassionate leave and unpaid family and domestic violence leave; Community service leave; Long service leave; Public holidays; Notice of termination and redundancy pay and the Fair work information statement.

The NES are minimum standards that cannot be overridden by the terms of enterprise agreements or awards. (Australia only) See ***the fair work commission (FWC), the fair work ombudsman (FWO).***

navigation bar: is a section at the top of your accounting software intended to help the user access information.

negative growth: is a contraction in business sales or earnings. It is also used to refer to a contraction in a country's economy, which is reflected in a decrease in its gross domestic product (GDP) during any quarter of a given year. See ***gross domestic product (GDP), recession.***

net amount: refers to the amount remaining after certain adjustments have been made for debts, deductions or expenses. Whereas gross refers to the total amount before anything is deducted.

net assets: the value of assets a company owns after the company has subtracted all liabilities form its total assets.

net loss: the *bottom line*, which shows a business loss that occurs when the business has more expenses than earnings during an accounting period.

net profit: the *bottom line*, which shows how much money the business *earns* after it deducts all its expenses. See ***profit.***

net realisable value: the market value of an inventory of goods or other assets less the costs of sale. **nil:** a balance that is zero or 0.00 is said to be a nil balance.

non-current asset: physical assets such as office equipment, land and buildings, computers and motor vehicles, that aren't expected to be converted into cash within the next twelve months.

non-current liability: anything that the business owes that isn't due to be paid out within the next twelve months, such as hire purchase debts and bank loans.

non-deductible expense: is an expense that income tax law does not allow as a tax deduction form your taxable gross income. A non-deductible expense does not reduce your tax bill. See ***deductible expense.***

non-operating expense: is an expense not related to a company's day to day business operations or manufacturing. Examples include costs for: lawsuit settlement payment, restructuring costs See ***operating expenses.***

non-operating income: income from a source that isn't part of a business's normal revenue-generating activities.

non-reporting entity: is where it has been determined that there are no users dependent on a general purpose financial report (GPFR) to gain an understanding of financial position and performance of the entity, and to make decisions based on the financial information contained in that report. In this situation, a non-reporting entity is permitted to prepare a special purpose financial report (SPFR) and not a GPFR. Small private companies are often a non-reporting entity. See ***special purpose financial report, reporting entity.***

notes to the financial statements: the section in the financial statements that offers additional detail about the numbers provided in those statements. The notes disclose more of the story behind the declared numbers. Notes to the financial statements are sometimes referred to as ***notes to the accounts.*** See **financial statements.**

CHAPTER 15

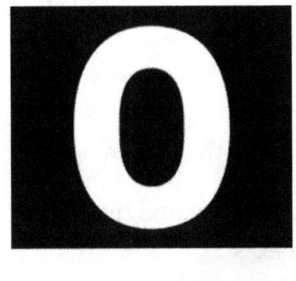

TERMS

ocr: optical character recognition (OCR) is the use of technology to distinguish printed or handwritten text characters inside digital images of physical documents, such as a scanned paper document. It can help in reducing time spent on data entry.

on account: the purchase or sale of goods and services on credit or partial payment of an amount owed. On account can also be referred to as *on credit*.

online accounting software: See *cloud accounting software*.

online banking: a method of banking in which transactions are conducted electronically through a bank or other financial institution's website. Online banking is also referred to as *e-banking, electronic banking, internet banking*. See *internet*.

opening balance: is the balance that is brought forward at the beginning of an accounting period from the end of a previous accounting period.

operating cash flow: cash generated by company operations to produce and sell company products.

operating expenses: are the day-to-day expenses a business incurs in order to keep it running, such as rent, office supplies, insurance. It does not include cost of goods sold (materials, direct labour, manufacturing overhead) or capital expenditures (building or machines). See *non-operating expenses*.

operating lease: is a contact that allows for the 'rental' of an asset from a lessor, but not under terms that transfer ownership of the asset to the lessee. Ownership of the asset is retained by the lessor during and after the lease term. See *finance lease*.

operating profit: is the profit from business operations (ie *gross profit minus operating expenses*) before deduction of interest and taxes.

opportunity cost: the value of a benefit forgone in favour of an alternative course of action. Every action has an opportunity cost because if you had not pursued course A you would have taken course B, which may or may not have provided a better return.

ordinary shares: also called fully paid ordinary shares (FPO), are the most common type of shares Holders of ordinary shares usually have the right to vote and participate in any dividends or distribution of assets on winding up of the company on the same basis as other ordinary shareholders. See *share, preference shares.*

ordinary time earnings: regular wages, not including irregular payments such as annual holiday leave loading, one-off bonuses and overtime. (Australia only).

other expenses: are expenses that are unrelated to the main focus of a business. Examples of other expenses include interest expense and losses on the sale of fixed assets.

other income: is income derived from activities unrelated to the main focus of a business. Examples of other income include interest income, rental income from sub-leasing unused office space, gains on the sale of fixed assets.

outstanding: not settled or paid.

overdraft: banks allow approved customers to overdraw past the balance in their current account with interest being charged on the overdrawn balance.

overdrawn: is the negative balance of a bank account when funds withdrawn exceed the funds available.

overhead costs: See *fixed costs.*

CHAPTER 16

TERMS

paperwork: is any task that involves many pieces of paper, such as handling papers, letters, paying bills, filing or filling out forms. Paper is becoming less common or reduced with 'paperwork' increasingly done electronically. See *paperless office.*

paperless office: or paper-free office is a work environment in which the use of paper is eliminated or greatly reduced. It is achieved by receiving or converting documents into digital form. The document is stored in an electronic filing cabinet or file and is easily retrievable. See *document management software.*

parent company: is a corporation that has *subsidiaries*, which are *wholly or partially-owned separate businesses* controlled by the parent. A parent company must usually have *at least 50% of a subsidiary's voting shares* for control of operations and management. A *wholly-owned subsidiary* is one in which the *parent owns 100%* of the stock. See *holding company, consolidated financial statements.*

partnership: two or more individuals who have joined together to carry on a business, sharing in risks and profits. The profits are shared in agreed proportions and each partner is liable for the partnership's debts.

partnership agreement: See *partnership deed.*

partnership deed: is a document that details the rights and responsibilities of each partner to a business operation. For example, a partnership deed could specify how profit from the partnership's business is to be divided among the partners. A partnership deed helps to avoid conflict which may arise between partners. A partnership deed is also referred to as a *partnership agreement.*

passcode: is a one-time, time-based numeric code that is used as an extra security step during the login process. See *two-step authentication (2SA).*

passphrase: is a password composed of a sentence or combination of words (and/or numbers) that are easy to remember. By using a longer password such as a passphrase and adding upper case letters and complex characters like symbols, they are more secure and much harder for a computer to crack. At least 16 characters is preferred, as the longer your password, the harder it is to guess.

An example of a passphrase is ILOVEtoReadWeLikeSecurity@! (it is not recommended to use this published example as your passphrase).

password: a secret string of characters used to verify the user to allow access to a computer system or service. Single word passwords, for example, 'sunshine' are easy to crack and don't offer appropriate security. Passphrases can offer more security. See ***passphrase.***

payables: an invoice that is due to be paid is called a payable and is included on the list of accounts payable. See ***accounts payable.***

pay as you earn (PAYE): individuals who earn wages or salaries have income tax (PAYE) deducted from each pay by their employer. The employer is responsible for passing this deduction on to the government. (Australia only).

payee: is the person who receives the payment when the cheque has been cashed by the bank. See ***cheque.***

PAYG instalments: are regular payments a business makes throughout the year (usually quarterly) towards its expected annual income tax liability. They help reduce the chance of having to make a large tax payment after lodging the tax return (Australia only).

PAYG payment summary: a summary issued to each employee of wages earned and tax deducted, due by 14 July each year. However, if you are using Single Touch Payroll (STP) to report all information, payment summaries are no longer required as your employees will see the information reported through STP via an employment income statement in their myGov account. *(Australia only)* See ***single touch payroll.***

PAYG payment summary annual report: is an *annual report*, which if using paper forms consists of a completed *PAYG payment summary statement*, the ATO original of *payment summaries* issued and is due by 14 August each year. This summary can also be lodged online. However, if you are using Single Touch Payroll (STP) to report all information, a

PAYG payment summary annual report is no longer required. *(Australia only)* See **single touch payroll.**

paypal: is a popular online service that enables an individual or business to pay, send money and accept payments. Users need to set up a PayPal account to access this service.

payroll: is a list of all the employees of a business, but the term is commonly used to refer to the total amount of money that a business pays to its employees, the business's records of its employees salaries and wages, bonuses and tax withheld.

payroll tax: is a state and territory tax assessed on businesses with larger payrolls, when the total wage bill of an employer (or group of employers) exceeds a threshold amount. The payroll tax rates and thresholds vary between states and territories. (Australia only).

PC: is still an abbreviation for a personal computer. However, in most cases PC is referring to the IBM-compatible type of computer. While a Mac is considered a personal computer, it is not a PC when referring to a specific type of computer. Hence the term **PC or MAC.**

PC or MAC: Computers used are either PC (IBM Compatible) or Apple Macintosh compatible. *Macs* run on the *MacOS X* operating system and the majority of PCs are sold with *Windows* installed in then. See **PC.**

penalty: the tax office and other government departments have numerous provisions which impose penalties on a taxpayer for failure to perform a specific act, file returns or omitting vital information on a return.

period end: is the period (or month) end date used to report your business activity.

periodic method: an accounting method of recording stock where you don't account for cost of goods sold with every sale, but instead only account for cost of goods sold and stock on hand when you do a stocktake at the end of a financial period. Purchases of stock during the year are recorded as expenses at the time of the purchase. Using the periodic method the cost of goods sold equals the beginning inventory plus purchases less ending inventory. See *stock, stocktake, inventory, perpetual method.*

perpetual method: an accounting method where you record the cost of goods sold with every sales transaction, and keep track of the current balance of inventory on a day-to-day basis. Using the perpetual method levels of stock are recorded and updated with every transaction. A stocktake is performed at the end of a financial period to compare records to the physical stock on hand. See *stock, stocktake, inventory, periodic method.*

personal loan: a type of loan available from banks, finance companies and other financial institutions. Funds are advanced (lent) to the customer for a fixed period, at a variable or fixed rate of interest with repayments calculated at the outset on the basis of monthly instalments.

petty cash: a small amount of cash, kept in a safe place, used for making small purchases such a milk, stamps etc. All money paid out must be recorded (usually in a *petty cash book*) so that the expenses can be included in the accounts.

petty cash book: a cash book to record small day to day/occasional cash expenditures.

physical capacity: the number of facilities a company has and the amount of product the company can manufacture.

posted: See *entered.*

power of attorney: a legal document in which one person gives legal authority to another to act on matters on their behalf.

preference shares: usually give their holder a priority or 'preference' over ordinary shareholders to payments of dividends or on winding up of the company. There are different kinds of preference shares with different rights and characteristics. See *shares, ordinary shares.*

prepayment: an expense paid for in advance or a deposit made against an invoice. A prepayment is reported as an asset and becomes an expense once the benefit has been received. For example: prepaid insurance, subscription services.

prepopulate: when you enter text into a form online, a text box, or a field, some of the information has already been automatically entered (or 'prepopulated') by the system. For example, on creating a new invoice in accounting software, the invoice number field is prepopulated.

price-to-earnings (P/E) ratio: helps investors determine the market value of a stock as compared to the company's earnings. For example. a high P/E could mean that a stock price is high relative to earnings and possibly overvalued. P/E ratio is calculated as follows:

$$P/E = \frac{\text{Market Price per Share}}{\text{Earnings per Share (EPS)}}$$

The price-to-earnings (P/E) ratio is also sometimes known as the *P/E ratio, P/E or PER*. See *earnings per share (EPS).*

prime cost depreciation: the depreciation method where the cost of the asset is spread *evenly* over the number of years of the asset's effective life. Prime cost depreciation is also referred to as *straight-line depreciation.*

principal: the face value amount of the loan, on which interest is calculated.

private company: See *company.*

private sector: the activities within an economy that are operated by and undertaken by private individuals, rather than by government. See *public sector.*

product: goods or services that can be offered to a market to satisfy the desire or need of a customer. In retailing, products are often referred to as merchandise, and in manufacturing, products are bought as *raw* materials, processed and then sold as finished goods.

professional accounting bodies: in Australia, there are three legally recognised professional accounting bodies which accountants can belong to: the Institute of Public Accountants (IPA), CPA Australia (CPA) and Chartered Accountants Australia and New Zealand (CA ANZ). Membership with any of these accounting bodies indicates that member has a high professional competence and accountancy knowledge. There are different levels of membership offered within each, based on the members experience and qualifications.

professional bookkeeping associations: in Australia, the following professional bodies offer membership for bookkeepers: Institute of Certified Bookkeepers (ICB), Association of Accounting Technicians (AAT), Australian Bookkeepers Association (ABA). Some offer different levels of membership, based on the members experience and qualifications.

profit: the accounting term for what is left from income (revenue) after expenses have been paid. See *gross profit, operating profit, net profit.*

profit and loss statement: shows the company's income (revenue) and expenses for a particular period of time. Expenses are deducted from income to arrive at net income or net loss (profit or loss) for a particular period of time. Other names for the profit and loss statement include *P&L, income statement, earnings statement, revenue statement, statement of comprehensive income, operating statement, statement of operations* and **statement of financial performance.**

proprietary limited company: See *company.*

provision: an adjustment for expenses or income not yet billed for where the exact amount is uncertain.

public sector: the part of the economy which is not privately owned and is controlled by the government.

publish: the act of transferring auto extracted data from a document to your online accounting software. See *document management and data extraction software.*

purchase: obtaining goods or services for a price either with cash or on credit.

purchase invoice: an invoice received from the seller for the purchase of goods or services. See *sales invoice, invoice, tax invoice.*

purchases journal: a special journal used to keep track of the *purchases* of items that the business has purchased *on account (credit)*. See **special journals.**

purchase order: a business may complete a purchase order when it needs to buy an item from a supplier. It can include details of the types, quantities and agreed prices for products and services. It is used to control the purchasing of products and services from external supplies.

purchases returns and allowances journal: a special journal used to keep track of the *returns* of items that a business has purchased *on account (credit)*. See **special journals.**

CHAPTER 17

TERMS

quarter: three month intervals of the year.

quarterly reports: financial statements prepared every quarter. See *interim financial statements.*

quick assets: assets that are or are expected to be *converted into cash* in the *near term* such as accounts receivable, short-term investments.

quick create icon: the plus + button provided in most online accounting software menus that allows the user to quickly and easily create an invoice, bill, contact, quote, purchase order and other types of entries.

quick ratio: See *current ratio.*

quote: a business can shop around and ask for suppliers to provide a written cost for goods or services – this is a quote. The business may choose the supplier who provided the best quote. Quotes are usually only valid for a certain time frame, a few weeks or months.

CHAPTER 18

TERMS

radio button: allows a user to choose a single option from a list of two or more options. A hollow circle represents a 'deselected' radio button which changes to a circle with a dot inside when 'selected'.

ransomware: using ransomware, cybercriminals infiltrate your device, lock and then demand money form you to unlock the files. There's no guarantee you'll get your data back if you pay the ransom. See ***cyberattack.***

ratios: calculations that look at the relationship between one financial figure with another and from the results, arrive at conclusions about the financial state of the business.

raw materials: are materials or substances that a company uses to manufacture its finished goods.

real time: whereby, information is sent to users as soon as it becomes available, or is happening 'live'.

real time accounting: with the use of online accounting software gives users the information they need, when they need it, as soon as a transaction is complete. See ***real time.***

realise: to turn a change in value from potential to actual, usually by selling an asset. For example, an investor whose share portfolio is increasing in value will realise a profit on the sale of her securities.

receipt: when payments are received from customers, the supplier can issue a receipt to confirm the details of the payment received. A receipt is proof that the payment has been made.

receivables: money that the business expects to receive for the payment for goods or services it has provided. The accounts that are due to be paid by the customers of a business are listed on the accounts receivable report. See ***debtors, trade debtors, accounts receivable.***

receivership: a type of bankruptcy in which a company can avoid liquidating itself and instead work with an appointed trustee to restructure its debt so it can emerge from bankruptcy. A receivership is a remedy available to secured creditors to recover amounts outstanding under a secured loan in the event the company defaults on its loan repayments.

recession: is an economic cycle contraction when there is significant decline in economic activity. Recessions generally occur when there is a widespread drop in spending which may be triggered by various events. In Australia, a recession is defined as a negative economic growth (decrease in its gross domestic product (GDP)) for two consecutive quarters. Governments usually respond to recessions by increasing money supply, increasing government spending and decreasing taxation. A recession is also referred to as an *economic recession.* See *economic cycle, gross domestic product (GDP), negative growth.*

recognise: to record a revenue or expense in a company's books.

reconciliation: the accounting process of matching one set of figures or documents with another set of figures or documents to ensure figures are correct and in agreement. For example: when a business reconciles its bank account, it is reconciling the bank account balance in its general ledger, with the bank's information on the bank statement and investigating and fixing any differences.

recurring: a transaction that *repeats regularly* every week or month for the *same amount to the same account* is said to be a *repeating or recurring* transaction. Examples of a recurring transaction would be the monthly rent, insurance, subscriptions.

refer to drawer: used by banks when a cheque presented by the payee/beneficiary is returned, usually due to insufficient funds in the drawer account. Payment is suspended in the meantime. See *bounce.*

reference: a number or combination of numbers or letters that are used to identify each transaction following through to the journals and ledgers. Each financial transaction is allocated a unique reference that can be traced through the accounting system. For example: a purchase journal for a credit transaction may have the reference PJ101, Bill or INV depending on which accounting software is used.

refund: return money or provide a credit, typically to a customer who is not satisfied with goods or services bought.

registered office: is the official address of an incorporated company, association or any other legal entity. It will form part of the public record and is required in most countries where the registered organisation or legal entity is incorporated.

registered tax agent: is an individual or entity who provides tax services and is registered with the Tax Practitioners Board (TPB). Registered tax agents are the only people allowed to charge a fee to prepare and lodge a tax return. (Australia).

reimburse: an individual who buys something for the business with personal funds can be reimbursed by the business, i.e. paid back for that purchase.

related-party revenue: revenue that comes from a company selling to another entity where the seller controls how the company operates and makes a profit.

remittance advice: a document that is given to a supplier or received from a customer that lists what invoices are included in a payment made.

repairs expense: costs of *ordinary* maintenance that *does not improve* an asset.

reporting entity: a company or other entity where it is reasonable to expect that there are users dependent on a general purpose financial report (GPFR) to gain an understanding of financial position and performance of the entity, and to make decisions based on the financial information contained in that report. These users could be shareholders, members, employees, creditors, leaders or potential investors. For example: listed public companies, large private companies with external shareholders who have no access to financial information other than the annual financial report. See *general purpose financial report, non-reporting entity.*

reporting period: is the time range over which business transactions are accumulated into a set of financial statements. The reporting period is typically either for a month, quarter, or year. Organisations use the same reporting periods from year to year, so that their financial statements can be compared to the ones produced for prior years. A reporting period is also referred to as the *accounting period.* See *fiscal year.*

R Terms

residual: a lump sum payment payable at the end of the lease term that roughly equates to the value of the asset.

restate earnings: to correct "accounting errors" by changing the numbers originally reported to the general public.

restructure: to reorganise business operations by means such as combining divisions, splitting divisions, dismantling an entire division, or closing manufacturing plants.

retained earnings: *net income or loss* on the income statement *is added or subtracted* to retained earnings on the shareholders' equity section of the balance sheet, at the end of the reporting period.

return on investment (ROI): measures the gain or loss generated on an investment relative to the amount of money invested. Return on investment is usually expressed as a percentage and calculated by:

$$ROI = \frac{Net\ Profit}{Cost\ of\ Investment} \times 100$$

revenue: earnings, what a business makes in monetary terms from its activities. Not to be confused with profit, since expenses need to be deducted from revenue. Revenue is also referred to as *income.*

revenue recognition principle: is the accounting principle that states revenues should be recognised when they are earned or realised, no matter when cash is received.

risk: measurable possibility of losing or not gaining value.

rounding: the process of putting a number up or down to the nearest number.

royalties: payments a business makes for the use of intellectual property owned by another business or individual.

CHAPTER 19

TERMS

salary: is a fixed amount paid to an employee for their work. People on salaries do not earn overtime pay like a wage earner when working more than their standard hours.

sales: all goods or services sold to customers.

sales discount: a discount that is given to a buyer for early payment for a sale made on credit.

sales invoice: the *invoice* issued by the *seller* when goods or services are *sold*. It contains all the details of the sale including credit terms if the item has been sold on credit. It is recorded in the *seller's* accounting system as a *sales invoice*. The *buyer* will need to enter it into their accounting system as a *purchase invoice*. See **invoice, tax invoice, credit terms.**

sales journal: a special journal used to keep track of the *sales* of items that customers (debtors) have purchased *on account (credit)*. See **special journals**.

sales returns and allowances journal: a special journal used to keep track of the *returns* of items that customers (debtors) have purchased *on account (credit)*. See **special journals.**

sales tax: a tax levied on the sale of goods and services purchased, paid by the consumer and submitted by seller to the governing tax authority. Also called GST, VAT, HST.

save: to put information/data into a computer's memory or to a storage location.

scan: a term that describes the process of digitising an image, allowing it to be stored on or modified by a computer. The most common method of scanning is by using an optical scanner.

screen sharing: software that allows remote access to another user to see everything that you see, including what you are doing. If you enable a '*remote control*' function, the other user will then be able to control your mouse and keyboard from their computer to move, close files and windows, open apps and even restart the user's computer. Common uses of screen sharing are for online training and meeting-based videoconferencing. Screen sharing is also called **desktop sharing.**

screenshot: an image of the data displayed on the screen of a computer or mobile device.

secured creditor: has rights not only against the debtor personally but against specific assets of the debtor which the creditor may be able to sell if that is necessary to recover the amount of debt.

secured debt: is debt backed or secured by collateral to reduce the risk associated with lending, such as a mortgage. If the borrower defaults on repayment, the bank can sell the house and use the proceeds to pay back the debt. See *security, collateral.*

securities fraud: deceptive practice in the stock (shares) or commodities markets that induces investors to make purchase or sale decisions on the basis of false information, frequently resulting in losses. Securities fraud is also referred to as *stock fraud* and *investment fraud.*

security: as used in accounting in relation to:

i) *debt*, is a legal right against a particular asset belonging to another; for example, a lender holding a mortgage on a building as security on the loan between the two parties. A creditor without security has rights only against the debtor, not against any specific property. Sometimes called a *security interest.* See *collateral, lien, mortgage.*

ii) *negotiable instrument,* is a tradable financial asset of any kind. Examples include shares (stock), bonds, debentures, forwards, futures, options and swaps. See *financial asset.*

iii) *information security,* is securing information (documents and data) from unauthorised access, modification and deletion. See *password, passphrase, two-step authentication (2SA)* iv) *computer security,* is the protection of computer systems and information from harm, theft, and unauthorised use. It is the process of preventing and detecting unauthorised use of your computer system.

iv) *cybersecurity,* is the technologies, processes and practices designed to protect networks, devices, programs and data from attack, damage or unauthorised access. See *cyberattack.*

separate entity: an accounting concept that states the transactions related to a business must be recorded separately from those of its owners and any other business. Only transactions that affect the business are recorded.

For example: if a business owner purchased an asset, using their own money, for their personal use, the transaction is not related to the business and is not recorded. The separate entity concept is also referred to as the ***entity concept.***

server: is a computer or a program that process requests and deliver data or services *to another computer*, known as the *client, over a network*. Thus whenever computers share resources with client machines they are considered servers.

There are many types of servers, including web servers, mail servers, file servers, print servers and virtual servers. For example: web servers respond to requests from browsers running on client computers for web pages or other web based services and mail servers accept and store email and then provides it to a requesting client. See **cloud, computer network.**

shares: part of the ownership of a company. A *share* refers to a *single unit* of the *stock - capital raised by the company*. An individual or business who buys a portion of the company's capital becomes a *shareholder* in that company's assets. Shares are also referred to as **equity, capital, stock.** See ***ordinary shares, preference shares.***

share capital: refers to the funds a company receives from selling shares to the public. For example: a company that issues 1,000 shares at $50 per share receives $50,000 in share capital. Even if the value of the shares increases or decreases, the value of the share capital remains as what the company received from the initial sale, or $50,000. The *two major types* of share capital are *ordinary shares* and *preference shares*. See **ordinary shares, preference shares.**

shares outstanding: refers to *all shares of a corporation* that have been *issued, purchased and held* by its shareholders, but does not include any shares repurchased by a company. Shares outstanding is also referred to as

outstanding shares, outstanding stock. See ***issued shares, treasury stock.***

shareholders: the owners of a corporation. Shareholders are also referred to as ***stockholders.*** See ***share, stock.***

shareholders' equity: is the amount of money that would be returned to shareholders if all the assets were liquidated and all the company's debt was paid off. Shareholders Equity is found on the balance sheet and shows the financial health of a company.

Shareholders' Equity = Total Assets − Total Liabilities.

Shareholders' equity is also referred to as ***equity, owner's equity, shareholder funds.***

short-term borrowings or debt: debt that a company must repay within the next twelve month period.

single-entry accounting: an accounting system in which financial transactions are only entered once. This is usually within a *cash book* system and does not utilise journals and ledgers for the process of balancing. See ***cash book.***

single touch payroll (STP): is an Australian Tax Office (ATO) compliance regulation that requires employers to send employee *payroll information* including *salary, wages, PAYG withholding and superannuation* to the ATO *at the same time* as their *standard pay run.* This information will then be made available to employees through ***myGov*** allowing employees to track their year to date earnings and remittances in real time.

It became mandatory for all employers to use STP from 1 July 2019. Most online accounting software providers *offer payroll solutions* with single touch payroll compliance built in. See **myGov.** (Australia only)

sme: small and medium-sized enterprises (SMEs) are businesses whose employee numbers fall below certain limits. In Australia, a SME has fewer than 200 employees. Micro businesses have 1-4 employees, small businesses 5-19, medium businesses 20-199, and large businesses 200+.

soft copy: is an unprinted *electronic* document file that exists in any digital form on computers, mobile devices etc, whereas *hard copy* is a printed digital document file on paper.

software: or computer software is a program that enables a computer to perform a specific task, as opposed to the physical components of the system (computer hardware).

sole trader: a business that is owned and run by one person and in which there is no legal distinction between the owner and the business entity. A sole trader is also referred to as **sole proprietorship or proprietorship.**

solvency: a company's ability to pay all its outstanding bills and other debts.

source document: a business document that provides all relevant details about a financial transaction and thus are the source of information that is recorded in the accounting records.

Common *source documents* include quotes, purchase orders, delivery dockets, invoices, adjustment notes, remittance advices, deposit slips, receipts, bank statements. Source documents need to be kept (either paper or digital copy) as written evidence of a transaction in case of any queries, an ATO or other audit. In Australia business records including employee records are required to be kept for up to 7 years.

special journals: are all accounting journals except for the general journal. In contrast to a general journal, each special journal records transactions of a specific type, such as sales or purchases.

The most common special journals *include the sales journal, purchases journal, cash receipts journal and cash payments journal.* These journals are used to record specific types transactions and keep organised records outside of the general journal. Other special journals are the *sales returns and allowances journal* and the *purchases returns and allowances journal.*

The following table summarises the transaction type for each special journal:

Special Journal	Transaction Type
Sales Journal	All credit sales
Purchases Journal	All credit purchases
Cash Receipts Journal	All cash receipts (including cash, cheques, credit card or EFTPOS)
Cash Payments Journal	All cash payments (including cash, cheques, credit card or EFTPOS)
Sales Returns and Allowances Journal	Credit given to customers for return of goods purchased on credit, or other allowances
Purchases Returns and Allowances Journal	Credit allowed by suppliers for return of goods purchased on credit, or other allowances

See *sales journal, purchases journal, cash receipts journal, cash payments journal, sales returns and allowances journal, purchases returns and allowances journal.*

special purpose financial report (SPFR): are financial statements that only need to apply the measurement and recognition Australian Accounting Standards with limited disclosure. An entity defined as a non-reporting entity is required to prepare SPFR. See *non-reporting entity.*

stakeholder: is a party that has an interest in and can either affect or be affected by the business. The main stakeholders are its owners, investors, employees, customers, creditors and government.

stale cheque: depending on the bank, cheques expire three to six months after the date issued. If it has not been presented to a bank within this time it becomes a stale cheque and may not be honoured by the bank. See *cheque.*

statement: in accounting can refer to:

i) a financial statement such a profit and loss statement or a balance sheet.

ii) a statement of account. For example: a statement from a supplier of goods to their customer detailing all the invoices issued to the customer in that month.

iii) a bank statement showing all transactions and the closing balance.

statement of cash flows: is the financial statement that shows the flow of cash through the business. This statement details how cash flowed into the business and what it was spent on. The statement of cash flows is also referred to as the *cash flow statement.*

statement of changes in equity: shows the change in an owner's or shareholder's equity throughout an accounting period. The statement of changes in equity is also referred to as *statement of changes in owner's equity* for a sole trader, *statement of changes in partners' equity* for a partnership, *statement of changes in shareholder equity* for a company or *statement of retained earnings.*

statement of financial performance: See *profit and loss statement.*

statement of financial position: See *balance sheet.*

stock: in accounting can refer to:

i) the *goods on hand* which are to be sold to customers. In this situation stock means *inventory.*

ii) the *ownership shares of a corporation.* Companies raise capital by issuing stock.

See *inventory, shares.*

stock keeping unit (SKU): is a unique number assigned for each particular item of inventory and is used to track business inventory.

stocktake: the physical counting of items (goods on hand) at the end of a financial period to determine the value of stock on hand.

straight-line depreciation: See *prime cost depreciation.*

subsequent event: a material event that occurs after the end of the accounting period and before the publication of an entity's financial statements. Such events are disclosed in the notes to the financial statements. See *material event.*

subsidiary: a company of which more than 50% of the voting shares are owned by another corporation called the *parent company*. The subsidiary can be *wholly or partially-owned* by the parent company. A *wholly-owned subsidiary* is one in which the *parent owns 100%* of the shares. See **parent company.**

subsidiary ledger: are created to provide detailed information about certain general ledger accounts. The debtors' and creditors' subsidiary ledgers are not part of the general ledger. See ***control accounts.***

super guarantee: is a compulsory amount that an employer must pay into an employee's chosen super fund as part of their employment conditions. The super rate to be paid is calculated as a percentage of the employee's ordinary time earnings. Employers have *28 days after the end of each quarter* to make the super guarantee payment for their employees, to avoid penalties. Super guarantee is also referred to as ***superannuation guarantee, super guarantee contributions***. (Australia only). See ***default super fund.***

super guarantee charge (SGC): is an additional charge to employers who have not paid the super guarantee for their employees to the correct super funds by the due date. Along with paying the SGC, employers must also lodge an SGC statement with the ATO. Additional penalties can apply if this not lodged. (Australia only).

suspense account: is a general ledger account in which certain transactions are temporarily recorded. The suspense account is used because the correct general ledger account could not be determined at the time that the transaction was recorded. Once resolved the amount is transferred out of suspense to the correct account.

sync: short for synchronise, to match up or coordinate something with something else so that they move or work together. For example: accounting apps can be set up to be in *sync* with your online accounting software. To match your phone's contacts to the contacts on your computer is another example of sync.

CHAPTER 20

TERMS

T account: is a visual representation of the ledger journal of individual accounts, so called because these accounts resemble a 'T' shape. The name of the account is placed above the 'T'. *Debit* entries are recorded to the *left side of the 'T'* and *credits* to the *right side of the 'T'*.

For example: T-Account's, using double entry accounting to manually record the following transaction:

You buy a motor vehicle for $1,000 Cash

(no GST/sales tax in this example)

Journal entry:

DR	Motor vehicle account	$1,000	
CR	Bank account		$1,000

Journal entry posted to T accounts:

Motor Vehicle account

Car $1,000 |

Bank account

| Car $1,000

In a manual accounting system, columns for the date, reference, description and amount would need be completed, when posting journals to the T accounts. At the end of a day, the total balance for each 'T' account is manually totalled and is written at the bottom of the account.

In addition to the use in manual accounting, the T account is also a valuable training tool in double entry accounting, showing how one side of an accounting transaction is reflected in another account/s. See ***double entry accounting, account, journals.*** **tangible asset:** any asset that you can touch, such as cash, inventory, equipment or buildings.

tax: a compulsory contribution to government revenue, paid on an individuals' income, business profits, or added to the cost of some goods, services, and transactions. The government uses taxes to maintain and run the country.

tax avoidance: the use of lawful means to minimise a tax bill.

tax evasion: illegal attempts to avoid paying tax, for example by not accurately reporting all income, overstating deductions. See ***black economy.***

tax file number (TFN): is a unique nine-digit number issued by the Australian Tax Office (ATO), to individuals and organisations to increase the efficiency in administering tax and other Australian government systems such as income support payments. A business has both a TFN and an Australian Business Number (ABN). See ***Australian Business Number (ABN).***

tax file number declaration: a form to be completed by an employee that is used to determine the amount of tax to be withheld from salary or wage payments. (Australia)

tax haven: a jurisdiction which attracts business through low tax rates.

tax invoice: is an *invoice* from a supplier who is registered for GST. The invoice from a business registered for GST must be a Tax Invoice which *includes* the words 'Tax Invoice' (preferably at the top), the supplier's business name, ABN, date of invoice, description of items sold and the amount of GST payable or if the total payable includes GST. (Australia) See ***invoice, goods and services tax (GST).***

tax liability account: an account that tracks tax payments that a company has made or must still make.

tax loss: generally when the total deductions you can claim for an income year exceed the total of your assessable income for the year.

tax practitioners board (TPB): the authority responsible for the registration and regulation of bas agents and tax practitioners. (Australia).

tax year: the period used to compute a taxpayer's taxable income. It is an annual period that is either a calendar year, fiscal year or a fractional part of a year for which the return is made.

term deposit: money may be placed with a bank or other financial institution for a fixed term at a fixed rate of interest which remains unchanged during the period of the deposit. A term deposit is also referred to as a *fixed deposit*.

terms of credit: See *credit terms*.

the cloud: See *cloud*.

the fair work commission (FWC): *'Changes Awards/Agreements, Conciliates & Concludes Conflict'* It is Australia's national workplace relations tribunal, with the power to carry out a range of functions relating to employment.

The Fair Work Commission:

i) sets the safety net of minimum wages and employment conditions within Australia (National Employment Standards).

ii) determines changes to pay and conditions in industrial awards and registered agreements.

iii) hears unfair dismissal claims.

iv) deals with harassment and bullying claims.

v) makes decisions about industrial action.

vi) resolves collective and individual workplace disputes through conciliation, mediation and public hearings.

the fair work ombudsman (FWO): *'Educates & Investigates'* It is an independent statutory agency of the Government of Australia that serves as the central point of contact for free advice and information on the Australian national workplace relations system.

The Fair Work Ombudsman:

i) ensures compliance with the Fair Work Act, related legislation, Awards and Registered Agreements.

ii) educates individuals and companies on pay rates and workplace conditions.

iii) appoints Fair Work Inspectors.

iv) provides advice and investigations in relation to problems with pay, conditions, entitlements, discrimination, performance management, policies and procedures.

TFN: See *tax file number*.

time-billing: is the process of taking data from an employee's time-sheet and charging it onto customers. The data is made up of the hours that the employee spent working on something for the customer, a description of the job and any other costs associated with the job.

title: the written evidence, such as a deed, that proves legal right of possession or control.

toolbars: are small graphical icons that act as a shortcut to execute a specific function or command. For example: a printer icon means it is a printing command, a diskette icon relates to the saving and storing files. They are typically located at the top of an application. See **menu bar.**

trade creditors: the money that <u>you owe</u> to suppliers. They're also referred to as creditors, trade payables, payables or accounts payable. See **accounts payable.**

trade debtors: the money which is <u>owed to you</u> by your *customers*. They're also referred to as *debtors, receivables* or *accounts receivable*. See **accounts receivable.**

trademark: distinctive name, symbol, motto, or emblem that identifies a product, service or company.

transaction: is a business event having a monetary impact on the financial statements of a business. Transactions are recorded in the accounting records of the business. Examples include the sale and purchase of goods and services, borrowing funds from a lender, income from investments, purchase of an investments, purchase of a business, disposal of a fixed asset, bank fees, etc.

transaction trail: is a list of all business transactions that occurred within a particular time frame. See ***audit trail.***

transfer: the allocation of funds from one account to another. This could be for a ledger account or a bank account. See ***electronic funds transfer (EFT).***

treasury stock: is stock which is bought back by the issuing company, reducing the amount of *shares outstanding* on the open market. An example of a motive for stock repurchase is to protect the company against a takeover treat. Treasury stock is also called ***reacquired stock.***

trial balance: an accounting report listing the debit and credit *balances* of all *general ledger accounts* at any point in time.

trust: is a structure where a trustee carries out the business on behalf of the trust's members (or beneficiaries). A trustee may be an individual or a company.

two factor authentication (2FA): an extra step to a log-in process that makes it significantly harder for someone to get access to your account, even if they have somehow managed to get hold of your password. It combines a something you *know* (password), with something you *have*, such as using an authenticator app on your phone to provide a temporary access code. This code is entered, in addition to your password at log in. Other names for similar processes that all add another layer of security are ***two-step authentication (2SA), two-factor or multi-factor authentication (MFA), two-step verification (2SV).*** See ***authenticator app.***

CHAPTER 21

TERMS

unaudited financial statements: financial statements which have not undergone a detailed audit examination by an independent qualified auditor.

uncleared funds: funds that have been credited to a beneficiary's account but which are not yet available for withdrawal. See ***cleared funds.***

unearned income: payment received for services which have not yet been performed.

undeposited funds: is an asset account used as a clearing account for money that has been received but not yet deposited into the business bank account.

For example, the business may receive cash and cheques from different customers in one day. The business codes these receipts to the relevant accounts (eg payment of a customer invoice, cash sale etc) and as the payment receipts are not yet banked, code the payment receipt to undeposited funds.

For banking, the business will total up the payments received, write out a deposit slip showing the total and take all to bank to deposit.

Once the deposit shows on the bank statement, the business can *transfer* it from the undeposited funds account to the bank account. Most accounting software has the option of clicking on a 'transfer' button for this. See ***clearing account.***

unlimited liability: refers to the full legal responsibility that general partners and sole traders assume for all business debts if the business can't pay its liabilities. This liability is not capped, and obligations can be paid through the seizure and sale of owners' personal assets, which is different than the limited liability business structure. See ***limited liability.***

unfranked dividends: company profits paid to shareholders which *have no tax credits* attached to the dividend. See ***imputation credit, franked dividends.***

uniform resource locator (URL): is a unique identifier used to locate a resource on the internet. It can be thought of as the *address of a resource* such as a website address, such as https://www.myweb.com. URL is also referred to as a **web address.**

uploading: data is being sent form your computer to the internet. It is the process of moving digital files such as photographs, documents or some other data, form your computer and placing them on to a central server so that someone else can retrieve them or to a website so others can see them. See *downloading.*

unpresented cheques: are cheques that have been sent to a supplier but have not yet been debited out of the bank account. This term is most often used in bank reconciliations.

unrealised gains or losses: is an increase/decrease in the value of an investment (or other asset) that is not yet sold for cash. Unrealised gains or losses are also called *"paper profit" or "paper loss".* A gain or loss becomes realized when the investment (or other asset) is actually sold.

unsecured loan: a loan to a company or individual who provides no collateral, so that the lender is entirely dependent on the borrower's capacity and willingness to repay. In the event of a default, the lender has a claim on the borrower's assets but will need to go through a legal process toe exercise it.

CHAPTER 22

TERMS

variable costs: are costs that increase or decrease as the quantity of the goods or services that a business produces changes. They rise as production increases and fall as production decreases. Examples of variable costs include the costs of raw materials and packaging. See ***fixed costs.***

variable rate loan: a loan in which the *interest rate* charged on the outstanding balance varies as market interest rates change. As a result, your payments will vary as well.

vendor: sells goods and services to customers.

virtual private network (VPN): is programming that creates an encrypted connection allowing users to send and receive data across public networks as if their devices were directly connected to a private network.

voluntary administration: is the process where a voluntary administrator is appointed, usually by a company's directors who have decided that the company is insolvent or likely to become solvent. The voluntary administrator will assess all the options available, and generate the best outcome for the business owner and creditors. See ***bankruptcy, involuntary administration.***

voluntary bankruptcy: see ***bankruptcy.***

voluntary liquidation: is a self-imposed wind-up and dissolution of a company that has been approved by its shareholders. It happens when a company has decided it has no reason to continue operating and wants to wrap-up its financial affairs including paying back creditors. It is not ordered by the court (not compulsory). Voluntary liquidation is also referred to as ***voluntary winding up.*** See ***liquidation.***

CHAPTER 23

TERMS

wages: a payment made to an employee for the hours worked. It is calculated by the agreed pay rate per hour, multiplied by the number of hours worked.

white-collar crime: is a crime committed to obtain or avoid losing money, property or services, or to secure a business advantage. Examples include securities fraud, embezzlement, money laundering.

wholly-owned subsidiary: is a company in which the parent company owns 100% of its shares. See *subsidiary, parent company.*

withdrawal: when funds are taken out of a bank account they are withdrawn.

withholding tax: is an income tax withheld or deducted from income due to the recipient and paid to the government by the payer of the income rather than the recipient of the income. Withholding tax usually applies to employee's wages, payments of interest or unfranked dividends or where the recipient does not quote a Tax File Number (TFN) or Australian Business Number (ABN).

window dressing: arranging financial details, such as deposits, loans and portfolios, to give the best possible impression for balance sheet purposes.

work in progress (WIP): refers to partially completed goods that are still in the production process. It is measured at the end of an accounting period, in order to assign a valuation to the amount of inventory still in production. Work in progress is also referred to as *work in process.*

workers compensation insurance: is insurance to cover employees in the event that they suffer a work-related injury. It is intended to include cover wages, medical expenses, treatment and rehabilitation costs. Workers Compensation Insurance is compulsory in Australia.

working capital: is the difference between a company's current assets minus its current liabilities. This figure represents a company's ability to pay its current liabilities with its current assets.

working capital ratio: See *current ratio*

worksheet: a type of working paper used by accountants as a preliminary step in the preparation of financial statements.

write down: to reduce the book value of an asset when its fair market value has fallen below its book value. Accounts that are commonly adjusted down include the company's goodwill, accounts receivable and long-term assets. See *impaired asset, fair market value.*

written-down value: the original cost of an asset less how much has been claimed so far in depreciation. Written down value is also called *book value or net book value.* See *book value.*

write-off: to eliminate the book value of an asset or liability. This would happen if a company or individual were to find it impossible to recover a debt.

write-up: to increase the book value of an asset because its book value is less than its *fair market value (FMV)*. A write up can occur if a company is being acquired and its assets and liabilities are restated to fair market value or if an earlier write down in its value was too large. See *fair market value.*

CHAPTER 24

TERMS

x-axis: is a horizontal axis on a graph. An example of an x-axis is the line across the bottom of a chart. The x-axis and its partner, the y-axis, tell us what data presented in the graph represents.

CHAPTER 25

TERMS

y-axis: is the vertical line in a graph. An example of a y-axis is the axis that runs up and down on a graph. The y-axis and its partner, the x-axis, tell us what data presented in the graph represents.

year-end: is the **E**nd **O**f the company's **F**inancial **Y**ear (EOFY). The end of the financial year is an important time for small businesses, completing bookkeeping, accounting, preparation of the year end financial statements, tax returns and planning for the new financial year.

year-end rollover: is the conversion of the general ledger from one fiscal accounting year to the next and occurs at the end of the fiscal year. The year-end rollover zeros off the profit & loss accounts and posts the resulting profit or loss to the retained earnings account.

yield: return on an investment that an investor receives over a particular period of time from dividends or interest expressed as a percentage of the cost of the investment.

The formula for calculating the yield is:

$$Yield = \frac{Net\ Realised\ Return}{Principal\ Amount} \times 100$$

CHAPTER 26

TERMS

zero: nil, no quantity, nought, the number 0.

zero based account (ZBA): a bank account that's always kept as close to zero as possible.

zero based budget (ZBB): rather than the previous year's budget being the starting point for the next budget, a zero-based budget assumes no activities, everything in the budget must be justified for each new period.

ABOUT THE AUTHOR

Karen Matthews is a Qualified Accountant, Bookkeeper, Registered BAS Agent, Xero Certified Partner, Intuit QuickBooks Certified ProAdvisor Online, Intuit QuickBooks Certified ProAdvisor (Advanced) Online, Dext (previously Receipt Bank) Partner and a Hubdoc Certified Advanced Partner.

She manages a company offering accounting, bookkeeping, training and technology solutions for small to medium businesses. With over twenty-five years accounting experience, Karen has a passion for technology and helping her clients achieve their business goals. Clients relate to her friendly approach and can-do attitude.

In addition to "The Easy Guide to Accounting and Bookkeeping Terms for Small Business", she has written bookkeeping and software training courses.

Karen has degrees in Commerce and Science from the University of Auckland and completed Australian taxation studies at Griffith University (Queensland). She is a Fellow of the Institute of Public Accountants (Australia) FIPA and the Institute of Financial Accountants FFA.

She lives with her family in Queensland, Australia.

LET'S GET SOCIAL
CONNECT WITH US ON

WEBSITE: www.mybusinesspod.net

FACEBOOK: http://www.facebook.com/mybusinesspod

TWITTER: http://www.twitter.com/mybusinesspod

INSTAGRAM: http://www.instagram.com/mybusinesspod

BIBLIOGRAPHY

Amadeo K 4 March 2019 The Black Economy and Its Impact. Accessed September 2019 through https://www.thebalance.com/black-economy-4173517

Australian Accounting Standards Board (2019) About the Australian Accounting Standards Board Accessed 30 September 2019 through https://www.aasb.gov.au/About-the-AASB.aspx

Australian Bureau of Statistics (2019) About the Australian Bureau of Statistics. Accessed 30 September 2019 through https://www.abs.gov.au/about?OpenDocument&ref=topBar

Australia Competition and Consumer Commission (2019) About Us. Accessed 30 September 2019 through https://www.accc.gov.au/about-us/australian-competition-consumer-commission/about-the-accc

Australian Cyber Security Centre Australian Government Stay Smart Online (2019) Two factor Authentication. Accessed 4 October 2019 through https://www.staysmartonline.gov.au/protect-yourself/do-things-safely/two-factor-authentication

Australian Securities and Investment Commission, (2019) Our Role ASIC. Accessed 17 September 2019 through https://asic.gov.au/about-asic/what-we-do/our-role/

Australian Taxation Office (2019) Fringe Benefits Tax. Accessed 14 October 2019 through https://www.ato.gov.au/General/Fringe-benefits-tax-(FBT)/

Australian Taxation Office (2019) GST. Accessed 15 October 2019 through https://www.ato.gov.au/Business/GST/

Australian Taxation Office (2019) Luxury car tax. Accessed 12 October 2019 through https://www.ato.gov.au/business/luxury-car-tax/when-lct-applies/

Australian Taxation Office (2019) Do you need to pay payroll tax? Accessed 14 October 2019 through https://www.ato.gov.au/Newsroom/smallbusiness/Employers/Do-you-need-to-pay-payroll-tax-/

Australian Taxation Office (2019) Types of Fringe Benefits Accessed 14 October 2019 through
https://www.ato.gov.au/general/fringe-benefits-tax-(fbt)/types-of-fringe-benefits/

Australian Taxation Office (2019) Single Touch Payroll Accessed 10 October 2019 through
https://www.ato.gov.au/Business/Single-Touch-Payroll/

Australian Taxation Office (2019) Super for Employers. Accessed 10 October 2019 through
https://www.ato.gov.au/Business/Super-for-employers/

Australian Taxation Office (2019) PAYG Withholding Accessed 15 October 2019 through
https://www.ato.gov.au/Business/PAYG-withholding/

Burkett D, 19 December 2017 Digitisation and Digitalisation, what means what? Accessed 19 September 2019 through
https://workingmouse.com.au/innovation/digitisation-digitalisation-digital-transformation.

Choudary A (2019) 7 steps to creating the perfect app-stack. Accessed 17 September 2019 through
https://www.edureka.co/blog/what-is-computer-security/

Cisco (2019) Common Cyberattacks. Accessed 18 September 2019 through
https://www.cisco.com/c/en/us/products/security/common-cyberattacks.html

Editor (5 May 2016) Forget about passwords: you need a passphrase. Accessed 14 October 2019 through
https://www.welivesecurity.com/2016/05/05/forget-about-passwords-you-need-a-passphrase/

Gilfillan, G (2015) Definitions and data sources for small business in Australia; a quick guide. Accessed October 2019 through
https://www.aph.gov.au/About_Parliament/Parliamentary_Departments/Parliamentary_Library/pubs/rp/rp1516/Quick-Guides/Data

GIO (2019) Workers compensation. Accessed 19 October 2019 through
https://www.gio.com.au/business-insuracne/workers-compensation/html

Bibliography

Jolly W (21 June 2018) What is a credit rating or credit score? Accessed 19 September 2019 through https://www.canstar.com.au/credit-score.what-is-a-creidt-rating/

Maguire A (16 September 2019) 7 KPI meanings small business owners need to know. Accessed 14 October 2019 through https://quickbooks.intuit.com/r/financial-management/the-7-most-important-kpis-to-track-as-a-small-business/

Matthews K (2017) Bookkeeping Masterclass, pages 10-12, 16-24, 29, 39-51, 83-85, 88-99, 111, 122.

Mark T (2019) Difference between digital signature and electronic signature. Accessed 30 September 2019 through http://www.differencebetween.net/technology/difference-between-digital-signature-and-electronic-signature/

Moyle I Difference between fair work commission and ombudsman 22 Sept 2016. Accessed 28 September 2019 through https://www.employeemanual.com.au/whats-difference-fair-work-commission-ombudsman/

Nations D (14 August 2019) What's the difference between a Mac and a PC? Accessed 6 October 2019 through https://www.lifewire.com/what-is-a-mac-4155662

Tax Practitioners Board (2019) Who needs to register as a tax agent. Accessed 14 October 2019 through https://www.tpb.gov.au/who-needs-register-tax-agent

Tax Practitioners Board (2019) Who needs to register as a bas agent. Accessed 10 October 2019 through https://www.tpb.gov.au/who-needs-register-bas-agent

The Fair Work Commission (2019) National Employment Standards Accessed 12 October 2019 through https://www.fwc.gov.au/awards-and-agreements/minimum-wages-conditions/national-employment-standards.

The Fair Work Ombudsman (2019) The fair work commission and us what's the difference. Accessed 28 September 2019 through https://www.fairwork.gov.au/about-us/our-role/the-fair-work-commission-and-us-whats-the-difference h

The Treasury Australian Government (2016 ongoing) What is the black economy? Accessed 30 September 2019 through https://treasury.gov.au/review/black-economy-taskforce/what-is-the-black-economy

Intel (2019) PC or Mac ?The Big Debate.
Accessed 12 October 2019 through
https://www.intel.com/content/www/us/en/tech-tips-and-tricks/pc-vs-mac-the-big-debate.html

FREE Cash Flow Forecast Spreadsheet!!

Claim your FREE Cash Flow Forecast Spreadsheet template at
https://bit.ly/CashFlow-Spreadsheet

Knowing how much money you may have available month by month or in a few months helps with your accounting and business planning. The Free Cash Flow Forecast spreadsheet will enable you to set a forecast for a year.

The Excel accounting template will allow you to show the predicted money available. The income and expenses descriptions can be changed to suit your business.

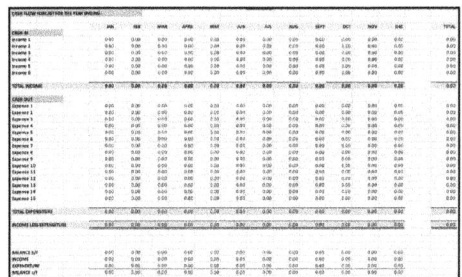

Claim your FREE Cash Flow Forecast Spreadsheet template at
https://bit.ly/CashFlow-Spreadsheet

Online Bookkeeping Course

*Would you like to Gain an understanding of the business books from Source Documents to Balance Sheet and see how all the 'pieces' fit together?

*Do you want to use these concepts to Gain a Greater Understanding of the accounting process 'happening behind the 'scenes' in a computerized accounting system, so that When you Record Transactions, you'll be More Aware of What you are Doing, Where your Financial Data goes in the System and What Reports you should be producing?

*Have you become the Bookkeeper by Default? Perhaps stressing out, not really understanding what you are doing or should be doing?

*Or just in need of a refresher course in Bookkeeping?

If you answered **Yes** to any of these questions, then this course has been created specifically for you.

Find out more about the Online Course 28 Days to Skyrocket Your Bookkeeping Skills at
http://bit.ly/BookkeepingSuperSpecialPlusBonuses

Notes

www.ingramcontent.com/pod-product-compliance
Lightning Source LLC
Chambersburg PA
CBHW071437160426
43195CB00013B/1944